THE IRISH POCKET
POTATO
RECIPE BOOK

Eveleen Coyle

Gill Books
Hume Avenue, Park West, Dublin 12

www.gillbooks.ie

Gill Books is an imprint of M.H. Gill & Co.

ISBN: 9780717166985

This book was created and produced by Teapot Press Ltd

Written by Eveleen Coyle
Edited by Fiona Biggs
Designed by Tony Potter
Picture research and photography by Ben Potter
Home economics by Imogen Tyler

Printed in Europe

This book is typeset in Garamond and Dax

A CIP catalogue record for this book is available
from the British Library.

5 4 3

Contents

Contents

Introduction

Ireland has a well-deserved reputation for the excellence of its produce, particularly potatoes which are consumed throughout the year. A superlative nutritional package, they are rich in vitamin C, vitamin B complex, potassium and fibre. They are gluten free and low in cholesterol; nothing beats a pot of floury spuds served with melting butter. Traditionally, potatoes are planted on St Patricks Day, 17 March, and are harvested thirteen to twenty weeks later.

The last fifty years have witnessed a sea change in our attitude to food and Irish cooking standards have vastly improved. Today the combination of cultural influences from immigration and foreign travel shape what we eat. Our ingredients are top class; we have excellent beef from cattle that are grass-fed all year round, mountain lamb from Connemara, Kerry and Wicklow, and the best dairy produce in Europe. And although we have embraced new styles of cooking, we still cherish our traditional recipes made with potatoes such as colcannon or boxty and use leftovers to make buttery potato cakes.

When the potato was first introduced to Ireland in the 17th century, it changed a whole way of life. It suited our soil and climate, flourishing in stony and boggy land in a way that corn and grain crops, so popular in the rest of Europe, did not. Potatoes were less vulnerable to coastal winds and yields were high. A tiny plot could feed a family and help pay the rent, so small farmers quickly became dependent on them.

By 1840 potatoes constituted one-third of the crops grown in Ireland. In 1845 potato blight hit Europe, spreading swiftly to Ireland where it swept through the country destroying crops. Over a million people died of famine and famine-related diseases between the years 1845–1852, and at least one and a quarter million emigrated. Over the next one hundred years, the population of the country halved.

Today the varieties of potatoes on the market are vast and increasing all the time, with many of the older types reappearing in local markets. As a nation, we tend to prefer floury potatoes such as Queens or Golden Wonders, which burst open looking for a bit of butter!

This book illustrates traditional cooking while acknowledging the various influences from home and abroad. Some of the recipes have appeared in my earlier book on potatoes but many others are new and have come from friends and favourite places, such as The Farmgate Café and Nash 19 in Cork, or Saba, Blazing Salads and The Pepper Pot in Dublin. All the recipes have been tested in a domestic kitchen; they work and they are delicious!

On our food walks (www.fabfoodtrails.ie) locals and visitors alike are always fascinated with the story of the potato in Ireland and we are continually asked for potato recipes. Here they are – enjoy!

BUYING AND STORING

🍂 Choose only the best quality potatoes and store them in a dark, cool, well-aired place.

🍂 Buy potatoes in small quantities and use them quickly.

🍂 Buy potatoes that have no damp patches or wrinkles and no visible green areas.

🍂 Remove the potatoes from plastic bags and store them in brown paper bags or bags made from natural fibres.

🍂 Potatoes bruise very easily so treat them as gently as you would apples.

COOKING TIPS

🍂 You should allow about 225 g/8 oz of potatoes per person, but you will probably need more if you are roasting them (roast potatoes are very simply delicious).

🍂 When deciding on cooking times and temperatures you need to take into account the size of the potatoes. If boiling them for mash, cut them up. Even if the potatoes are small, cut them in half – just one cut surface on each potato means that they will cook faster.

🍂 Preserve the flavour of new potatoes by steaming them instead of boiling them.

🍂 New potatoes should be added to boiling water, brought back to the boil and boiled until tender.

❧ There are differing opinions on whether potatoes ought to be covered or not during cooking. I don't cover them as a rule unless a recipe demands it.

❧ Cook potatoes in as little water as possible – the nutrients in the potatoes leach into the cooking water.

❧ With older potatoes, put them in a saucepan of lightly salted cold water and bring to the boil.

❧ A little fresh mint or a squeeze of lemon juice added to the cooking water prevents discoloration after cooking.

❧ It's best not to prepare potatoes in advance; if you have to, dry them and put them in a plastic bag in the bottom of the fridge to reduce discoloration. Do not leave them sitting in a pot of water.

❧ Unpeeled potatoes are much more nutritious and a lot less trouble to prepare. If you do peel potatoes, use a sharp vegetable peeler. Most of the potato's nutrition is just under the skin so you don't want to lose it.

❧ Cut away any green bits – these contain a toxin called solanine that can cause stomach upsets.

❧ Season to your own taste.

❧ For the purposes of the recipes in this book, unless otherwise stated, salt is sea salt, potatoes are old, cream is single cream and eggs and individual pieces of fruit and vegetables are medium.

COMMON VARIETIES AVAILABLE IN IRELAND

Potatoes tend to fall into three seasons or categories:

First Earlies available late May–July

Second Earlies available early July/late July–August

Main Crop available September–May

❧ Home Guard – a first early crop, white-fleshed potato. They are good for boiling, roasting, and new potato salads.

❧ Queens – second early, delicious floury potatoes, good for all uses. Usually available for just a short time from late June–August.

❧ Golden Wonder – dry, floury russet-skinned potatoes, one of the best of the late main crop potatoes (20 weeks).

❧ Kerr's Pink – another late main crop potato, mostly dry and floury with a pink skin, and available from late August.

❧ Records – main crop potato, dry and floury with yellow flesh.

❧ Rooster – main crop potato, good for most methods of cooking. Roosters now account for 60 per cent of the potatoes sold in Ireland, probably at the expense of some of the older favourites like Golden Wonder.

- Maris Piper – firm-fleshed potato, terrific for chips and for roasting.

- Cultra – white-skinned, cream-fleshed slightly waxy potato, very popular for home growing and a good all rounder.

- Orla – this is a second early with yellow skin. It is fast growing and popular with organic farmers around the country.

Field on the west coast of Ireland, still showing scars of potato ridges abandoned during the Great Famine of 1845–46.

SOUPS

Served as a snack, a starter or a dinner in itself, soup can be the best of meals or the most ordinary. A good home-made soup is nourishing, inexpensive, satisfying and makes an excellent base for many other soups. Just use lots of quality ingredients and a good stock base.

Fataí a chuirtear sa mBealtaine nó nuair a labhras an Chuach bíonn siad mall.
Potatoes planted in May or while the Cuckoo sings are late potatoes.

Irish Saying

INGREDIENTS

1 large onion,
chopped

2 tbsp butter or
bacon fat

200 g/7 oz potatoes,
peeled and chopped

900 ml/1½ pints
chicken or beef stock

125 ml/4 fl oz milk
or cream

salt and freshly
ground black pepper

chopped fresh
parsley, to serve

Potato Soup

This is a traditional soup recipe. Serve
it with various garnishes of your choice:
cheese, parsley, chives or streaky rashers
crispy fried and crumbled are all good. A
good stock improves the flavour.

METHOD

Sweat the onion in the butter, add the potatoes and cook for
10 minutes. Turn gently and frequently but do not allow them
to brown. Add the stock and simmer until the potatoes are
tender. Purée in the blender and add the milk. Reheat, check the
seasoning, stir in the parsley and serve.

SERVES 4

INGREDIENTS

3 tbsp butter

450 g/1 lb leeks, cut into 2.5-cm/1-inch pieces

450 g/1 lb potatoes, peeled and chopped

1.2 litres/2 pints chicken stock

salt and freshly ground black pepper

fresh crusty bread, to serve

Potato and Leek Soup

This simple soup, a less complicated hot version of Vichyssoise, makes the most of two easy-to-grow winter vegetables. A great lunch dish for a cold day, served with lots of fresh crusty bread.

METHOD

Melt the butter in a heavy-based saucepan and add the leeks. Cover with greaseproof paper and a tight lid. Sweat until the leeks are soft. Add the potatoes, cover and cook for a further 10 minutes, watching carefully so they do not burn. Add the stock and simmer for 30 minutes until the potatoes are cooked. Season well, liquidise and serve piping hot with fresh crusty bread.

SERVES 6

INGREDIENTS

4 tbsp butter

400 g/14 oz sorrel leaves, stalks removed

1 small onion, chopped

1 shallot, chopped

450 g/1 lb potatoes, peeled and diced

850 ml/1½ pints chicken stock

salt and freshly ground black pepper

croutôns and single cream, to garnish

Potato and Sorrel Soup

A really special soup with a terrific sharp flavour.

METHOD

Melt the butter in a heavy-based saucepan and add the sorrel. Cover and sweat until the leaves wilt and turn dark green. Add the onion and shallot, cook for 1–2 minutes, then add the potatoes and stock. Simmer for 40 minutes until the potatoes are cooked. Liquidise, then season to taste, garnish with croûtons and cream and serve.

SERVES 4

INGREDIENTS

2 tbsp butter

450 g/1 lb onions, peeled and chopped

225 g/8 oz potatoes, peeled and diced

1 tbsp chopped fresh parsley

850 ml/1½ pints chicken stock

150 ml/5 fl oz milk or top-of-the-bottle milk

salt and freshly ground black pepper

Potato and Onion Soup

This is a really handy recipe simply because most of us always have potatoes and onions in the house.

METHOD

Melt the butter in a heavy saucepan, add the onions and potatoes and coat well with butter. Add the parsley and seasoning. Cover tightly with greaseproof paper under the lid and leave to sweat for about 10 minutes until the potatoes are tender but not brown. Add the stock, bring to the boil, add the milk and boil gently until the potatoes are cooked. Season to taste with salt and pepper.

SERVES 4

INGREDIENTS

85 g/3 oz butter

900 g/2 lb potatoes, peeled and diced

¼ head of celeriac, diced

2 carrots, diced

900 ml/1½ pints chicken or vegetable stock, or water

1 leek, halved lengthways and sliced

1 onion, diced

300 ml/10 fl oz cream or cream and milk mixed (optional)

pinch of freshly ground nutmeg

85 g/3 oz smoked bacon

salt and freshly ground black pepper

croûtons and spring onion strips, to serve

Potato Soup with Bacon and Vegetables

This soup should be thick, chunky and rich. The smoked bacon sprinkled on top gives it a lovely flavour.

METHOD

Heat 55 g/2 oz of the butter in a heavy saucepan, add the potatoes, celeriac and carrots and sauté. Cover with stock, bring to the boil and simmer for about 40 minutes. Purée half the soup in the liquidiser. Heat the remaining butter in a saucepan, add the leek and onion and sauté lightly (be careful not to overcook or burn them), then combine with the purée and the remaining soup. Add the cream, season with the nutmeg and salt and pepper and cook for a further 5 minutes.

Dice the bacon and brown it in the butter-coated pan. Serve the soup with the croûtons, diced bacon and spring onion strips sprinkled on top.

SERVES 4-6

INGREDIENTS

knob of butter
1 small onion,
chopped
1 celery stick,
chopped
2 potatoes, chopped
2 garlic cloves,
roasted
1 litre/1¾ pints fish
stock
1 smoked trout fillet
2 long dill stems
4 tsp crème fraîche
salt and freshly
ground black pepper

The Pepper Pot Smoked Trout Potato Soup

A deliciously flavoured creamy soup that makes the most of a small amount of smoked trout.

METHOD

Heat the butter in a stock pot until foaming. Add the onion and celery and salt to taste, then stir, cover and cook until the onions are translucent, stirring occasionally. Add the potatoes and garlic and stir, then add the stock and a pinch of pepper. Simmer until the potatoes are just cooked, then blend in a liquidiser, adding additional liquid if necessary. Crumble the trout into bite-sized pieces and add to the soup. Snip the dill into the soup with a sharp scissors.

Serve in warmed bowls and top each portion with 1 teaspoon of crème fraîche.

SERVES 4

INGREDIENTS

900 ml/1½ pints
water

900 ml/1½ pints
stock

175 g/6 oz brown
lentils

175 g/6 oz potatoes,
peeled and finely
diced

2 carrots, diced

75 g/2¾ oz onions,
diced

3 celery sticks, diced

45 g/1⅔ oz fine
oatmeal, blended
with a little water

250 ml/9 fl oz milk

freshly ground
nutmeg, to taste

salt and freshly
ground black pepper

Winter Soup

This wonderful, old-fashioned cold-
weather soup is both filling and
nourishing, and is guaranteed to warm the
cockles of your heart.

METHOD

Put the water and stock into a saucepan and add the lentils and
potatoes. Bring to the boil, add the remaining vegetables, then
add the oatmeal. Bring back to the boil, stirring gently, then stir
occasionally until cooked – about 45 minutes. Add the milk and
seasoning. Liquidise the soup. Return to the pan and bring to
the boil again. Serve piping hot.

SERVES 6–8

INGREDIENTS

1 blade of mace
1 bouquet garni
2 tbsp bacon fat or butter
1 large potato, peeled and chopped
1 onion, chopped
1 carrot, chopped
3 celery sticks, chopped
1.7 litres/3 pints light stock
55 g/2 oz brown lentils, rinsed
30 g/1 oz ground rice
125 ml/4 fl oz milk
125 ml/4 fl oz cream
salt and freshly ground black pepper

Potato and Vegetable Soup

The mace in this recipe helps to bring out the flavours of the vegetables, lifting this otherwise very simple soup out of the ordinary.

METHOD

Add the mace to the bouquet garni. Melt the fat in a saucepan, add the vegetables, and toss. Cook gently until they have absorbed the fat but are not browned.
Add the stock and the lentils and simmer for 45 minutes.
Remove the bouquet garni and liquidise. Return to the saucepan and thicken with the ground rice. Season, bring back to the boil, add the milk and cream and serve.

SERVES 6

INGREDIENTS

225 g/8 oz dried
white haricot beans

3 litres/6 pints
water

1 large onion,
roughly chopped

2 celery sticks, sliced

1 carrot, sliced

6 tbsp olive oil

2 courgettes, sliced

4 tomatoes, peeled
and roughly chopped

4 large potatoes,
peeled and chopped

3 fresh borage
leaves, finely
chopped

225 g/8 oz dried
elbow macaroni

2 tbsp pesto sauce

6 tbsp grated
pecorino cheese

fresh crusty bread,
to serve

Minestrone and Potato Soup with Pesto

This soup takes some time to make but it's worth the effort. It calls for fresh borage which always tries to colonise the garden, so this is a good way to use up some of your crop.

METHOD

Soak the haricot beans overnight and partially cook in unsalted boiling water. Drain and put in a large saucepan with the water. Add the onion, celery, carrot and 4 tablespoons of the oil and simmer for about 1 hour. Add the courgettes, tomatoes, potatoes and borage. Bring back to the boil and cook for a further 30 minutes. Add the macaroni and cook for 15 minutes, or until the macaroni is tender but still firm to the bite. Stir in the pesto with the remaining oil, add the cheese and serve immediately in warmed dishes with good crusty bread.

SERVES 8

INGREDIENTS

170 g/6 oz potatoes, peeled and sliced

3 large leeks, white parts only, sliced

1 celery stick, sliced

2 tbsp butter

1.2 litres/2 pints chicken stock

150 ml/5 fl oz cream

salt and freshly ground black pepper

1 tbsp snipped fresh chives, to garnish

Vichyssoise

Not traditional to Ireland, perhaps, but very good and easy to make. Once more, try to use good stock. It makes a difference to the delicate flavour and creamy consistency of this soup. A stock cube just won't do!

METHOD

Sweat all the vegetables in the butter until just soft. It is a good idea to put a little greaseproof paper under the lid of the saucepan when sweating vegetables. They must be soft but not coloured, so keep your eye on them and stir occasionally. Stir in the stock, bring to the boil and simmer for about 15 minutes. Liquidise or rub through a sieve. The soup must be very smooth. Season and stir in the cream. Leave to cool, then whisk for a few minutes and chill. Serve sprinkled with chives.

SERVES 4

INGREDIENTS

1 tbsp olive oil

2 tbsp onion, finely chopped

1 garlic clove, finely chopped

450 g/1 lb potatoes, thickly sliced

2 pinches of saffron

900 ml/1½ pints vegetable stock or water

3-4 basil leaves, torn

3 Italian tomatoes, peeled

salt and freshly ground black pepper

4-6 strips of sun-dried tomatoes in oil

Provençal Potato Soup

This is a traditional recipe from France, but it is a welcome dish on an Irish table.

METHOD

Heat the oil in a saucepan, add the onion and garlic and sauté until they are transparent but not brown. Add the potatoes and cook over a medium heat, coating the potatoes with the oil. Add the saffron and leave for about a minute, then add the stock, basil leaves, tomatoes, and salt and pepper to taste. Simmer for about 20 minutes. Add a few strips of the sun-dried tomatoes and cook until the potatoes are tender.

SERVES 4

INGREDIENTS

2 tbsp butter

225 g/ 8 oz young leeks

450–900 g/1–2 lb tomatoes, peeled and chopped

450 g/1 lb potatoes, peeled and diced

750 ml/1¼ pints light stock or water

60 ml/2 fl oz cream or top-of-the-bottle milk

salt and freshly ground black pepper

chopped fresh chervil or basil, to serve

Potato, Tomato and Leek Soup

This is an unusual combination for a soup, but it is one that works very well, the leeks providing a milder and more subtle base than onions. A great winter warmer!

METHOD

Melt the butter in a heavy pan and cook the leeks gently until soft, then add the tomatoes and cook until the juice starts running. Toss in the potatoes, season and cover with the stock. Bring to the boil and simmer for about 20 minutes until the potatoes are cooked. Purée, check the seasoning, return to the pan and bring back to the boil slowly. Add the cream and serve at once, garnished with chervil.

SERVES 4–6

INGREDIENTS

chicken bones/
carcass/giblets
225 g/8 oz
vegetables, such as
carrots, leeks and
celery, chopped
1 onion, peeled and
sliced
6 peppercorns
bay leaf (optional)
salt

Chicken Stock

Stock is simple to make, costs just about nothing and is one of the most useful items to have in your freezer. I freeze it in an ice-cube tray and then put the cubes into bags; that way you can use as little or as much at a time without having to get out the ice-pick.

METHOD

If you are using the carcass, break it up, then chop the vegetables. Place all the ingredients in a saucepan, add enough water to cover, bring to the boil, skim if necessary and then simmer for about 1½–2 hours. Strain, leave to cool and skim the fat off. It is now ready to use. I don't use a bay leaf in chicken stock because I find the flavour too strong, but suit your own taste.

MAKES 1 LITRE/
2 PINTS

INGREDIENTS

450 g/1 lb shin beef cut into pieces

450 g/1 lb marrow bones

1 bouquet garni

1 onion, peeled and sliced

1 carrot, chopped

1 celery stick, chopped

salt

Beef or Brown Stock

This is an essential stock for meat-based soups (and stews). Full of nutritious marrow, it is so much better than ready-made beef stock and well worth making.

METHOD

Preheat the oven to 220°C/425°F/Gas Mark 7. Put the meat and bones in a roasting tin and brown them in the preheated oven for 30 minutes before adding them to the stock to improve the colour. Put all the ingredients in a saucepan and cover with water. Bring to the boil, skim and simmer for about 4 hours. Strain, leave to cool and then remove any fat from the top before using or freezing.

MAKES 1 LITRE/ 2 PINTS

INGREDIENTS

450–675 g/1 lb–
1 lb 8 oz fish bones
and trimmings
1 bouquet garni
1 onion, peeled and
sliced
salt

Fish Stock

Ready-made fish stock pales into insipid insignificance compared with this robust version, which will make all the difference to your home-made soups.

METHOD

Put the fish bones and trimmings in a stock pot, cover with 600 ml–1.2 litres/1–2 pints of water and bring to the boil. Before adding the other ingredients, skim off the top. Simmer for about 30 minutes and then leave to cool. Fish stock does not keep very long even in the fridge, so if you are not using it the same day it is best to freeze it.

**MAKES 1 LITRE/
2 PINTS**

INGREDIENTS

1 onion
1 carrot
3 celery sticks
vegetable trimmings
1 bouquet garni
salt
6 black peppercorns

Vegetable Stock

Most vegetable trimmings can go into vegetable stock so what I am suggesting here is just a guideline. Avoid brassicas though, as they are too strong and can sour the stock.

METHOD

Peel and chop the root vegetables and chop the celery sticks. Heat a little oil in a saucepan and gently fry the onion until soft. Add all the other vegetables, cover with water and bring to the boil. Simmer for about 2 hours. Strain and leave to cool.

**MAKES 1 LITRE/
2 PINTS**

OLD FAVOURITES

The problem with potatoes is that all too often little thought goes into their preparation. Although simple, they are often difficult to get just right. Firing potatoes into a hot oven around a lump of meat does not guarantee good roast potatoes – and lumpy mashed potatoes should be outlawed.

Prátaí ar maidin, prátaí ar nóin, is dá n'eireionn san oíche prátaí a gheobhainn.
Potatoes in the morning, potatoes at noon, and if I rise during the night potatoes is what I would get.

Irish Saying that reflects how much people ate potatoes in the past.

INGREDIENTS

900 g/2 lb potatoes

90 ml/3 fl oz top-of-the-bottle milk or half-milk and half-cream or milk

2 tbsp butter

salt and freshly ground black pepper

Traditional Mashed Potatoes

Choose floury old potatoes such as Kerr's Pinks, Golden Wonders or Records. Select potatoes of approximately the same size. Put them in a saucepan of lightly salted cold water and boil carefully, uncovered or partly covered, until they are cooked. If you can bear to peel hot potatoes, boil them in their skins – it does improve the flavour. If you can't, peel them first and boil them even more carefully as they tend to break up easily.

METHOD

Scrub the potatoes, bring them to the boil and cook until just done. While they are cooking, warm the milk and cream. Drain the potatoes, peel quickly and shake them over the heat to dry out. Mash them with a hand masher, adding the butter and the warmed milk and cream. Season to taste.

SERVES 6

INGREDIENTS

900 g/2 lb potatoes
2 tbsp fruity olive oil
90 ml/3 fl oz cream
or top-of-the-bottle
milk
salt and freshly
ground black pepper

Olive Oil Mash

The flavour of these is quite different from that of potatoes mashed with butter. The olive oil is all important. If you use oil the quality of car oil, the potatoes will taste of car oil, so use a good quality fruity oil for this recipe. It is very good with grilled or barbecued meat.

METHOD

Scrub the potatoes well, bring to the boil and cook until tender. Drain and peel the potatoes, add the olive oil, cream and salt and pepper to taste. Mash well together and taste for seasoning. Serve piping hot.

SERVES 6

INGREDIENTS

900 g/2 lb potatoes

2 tbsp butter, plus extra to serve

90 ml/3 fl oz top-of-the-bottle milk or half milk and half cream

8 tbsp chopped fresh parsley

8 tbsp snipped fresh chives

salt and freshly ground black pepper

Mashed Potatoes with Fresh Herbs

Make sure that your herbs are fresh and dry. If herbs are damp when you are chopping them they will bruise easily, and won't look very attractive when added to the hot mashed potato.

METHOD

Cook the potatoes in lightly salted boiling water until tender. Drain, peel and mash the potatoes, add the butter, cream and salt and pepper to taste and mash again. Beat in the parsley and chives with a wooden spoon. Taste for seasoning. Serve in a warmed bowl with a little melting butter in the centre.

Variations

Scallions, spinach (finely chopped) or streaky bacon rashers fried to a crisp all make a wonderful addition to mashed potatoes and can be used instead of the herbs suggested above. Choose carefully and don't mix too many flavours. Also bear in mind what you plan to serve with them.

SERVES 6

INGREDIENTS

900 g/2 lb potatoes
1 large fresh onion, finely chopped
1 tbsp sunflower oil
4 tbsp butter
1 tbsp chopped parsley
salt and freshly ground black pepper

Mashed Potatoes with Onions

This is a nice recipe, but it is essential to cook the onion until it is soft: a mouthful of uncooked onion is not pleasant in this dish.

METHOD

Cook the potatoes in lightly salted boiling water until tender. Meanwhile, soften the onion in the oil but do not allow it to brown. When the potatoes are cooked, peel and mash them well with the butter, and season to taste. Add the onion and parsley and mix well. Serve immediately in a warmed dish.

SERVES 4

INGREDIENTS

900 g/2 lb potatoes
225 ml/8 fl oz milk
4 tbsp extra virgin
olive oil
55 g/2 oz freshly
grated Parmesan
cheese
salt and freshly
ground black pepper

Mashed Potatoes with Parmesan and Olive Oil

Darina Allen is one of Ireland's best cooks and her *Simply Delicious* series has changed the way we look at food. This is one of her recipes from *Simply Delicious Versatile Vegetables*.

METHOD

Cook the potatoes in lightly salted boiling water until almost tender. Pour off most of the water, cover and steam for the rest of the cooking time. Boil the milk and add the oil to it. Mash the potatoes, add half the hot milk and oil mixture, the cheese and then the remaining milk. Season to taste. Make sure the potatoes are well mashed and light.

SERVES 4

INGREDIENTS

1.4 kg/3 lb good
floury potatoes,
peeled

olive oil

salt and freshly
ground black pepper

Roast Potatoes

Every family has the only recipe for really good roast potatoes and these are our favourite. We roast them the following way.

METHOD

Preheat the oven to 220°C/425°F/Gas Mark 7. Cook the potatoes in lightly salted boiling water, simmering with the lid off for 5 minutes. Drain and dry them off in the saucepan by holding them over the heat. Replace the saucepan lid and shake vigorously to roughen up the outside. Heat the oil in a roasting pan and add the potatoes; baste them all over and sprinkle with salt and pepper. Roast for about 45 minutes in the preheated oven, turning at least once. The outside will then be beautifully crisp.

If you use particularly floury potatoes for this recipe, they will disintegrate slightly and won't look like the perfect roast potato – but they taste luscious!

SERVES 6

INGREDIENTS

900 g/2 lb peeled
potatoes
hot oil or fat, for
roasting
salt and freshly
ground black pepper

Firm Roast Potatoes

This is a more sober roast potato. The outside is less crisp and the inside firm and well behaved. It tends not to fall apart in the roasting pan so looks good. The lesser quantity of potato used than in the previous recipe seems to feed the same number of people, which says it all. The same rules apply.

METHOD

Preheat the oven to 220°C/425°F/Gas Mark 7. Peel the potatoes and put them straight into the hot oil or fat, either around the meat or in a roasting tin on their own. Cook in the preheated oven for at least 45 minutes, basting and turning the potatoes a couple of times during cooking. Test with a skewer and sprinkle with salt and pepper just before they are cooked. Serve in a warmed bowl or arrange them on a large meat platter around the roast.

SERVES 6

INGREDIENTS

2 tbsp olive oil

2 tbsp butter

900 g/2 lb potatoes, well scrubbed

1 garlic bulb, separated into cloves, unpeeled

salt and freshly ground black pepper

Roast Potatoes with Garlic and Butter

Simple and good, the garlic loses its sharpness when it is roasted.

METHOD

Preheat the oven to 220°C/425°F/Gas Mark 7. Heat the oil and butter in a roasting tin in the preheated oven. Add the potatoes with a little salt and pepper. Roast for about 25 minutes, basting and turning once. Add the garlic and roast for a further 15 minutes, by which time the potatoes will be cooked through and brown. The garlic should be deliciously creamy and come away from the skin easily.

SERVES 6

INGREDIENTS

900 g/2 lb unpeeled potatoes, cut into quarters

4 tbsp hot oil

3 fresh rosemary sprigs

1 garlic bulb, cloves separated

salt and freshly ground black pepper

Roast Potatoes with Garlic and Rosemary

An Italian dish, these are particularly good with spring lamb or chicken.

METHOD

Preheat the oven to 220°C/450°F/Gas Mark 7. Toss the potatoes in the hot oil in a roasting tin, strip the rosemary sprigs and sprinkle the spikes over the potatoes with salt and a little pepper. Add the garlic to the tin and roast in the preheated oven for about 30 minutes, turning once. These potatoes are full of flavour – they smell irresistible and look terrific too.

SERVES 4

INGREDIENTS

1.4 kg/3 lb small even-sized potatoes
10–12 bay leaves
4 large garlic cloves, unpeeled
6 tbsp olive oil
salt and freshly ground black pepper

Roast Potatoes with Bay Leaves

Home Guard from the first early potatoes are great for this recipe, although any small and evenly sized potato will do. They are particularly good with game, and handy for entertaining. You can parboil and prepare them with the bay leaf in advance, then put them in the oven when it suits you.

METHOD

Preheat the oven to 220°C/ 425°F/Gas Mark 7. Cook the potatoes in lightly salted boiling water for 3–4 minutes, then drain and leave to cool slightly. Carefully cut a slit in half of the potatoes and insert a bay leaf in each. Meanwhile, place the garlic and oil in a large roasting tin and place in the preheated oven for a few minutes until the oil is hot. Add the potatoes and make sure they are well coated in the oil. Season with salt and pepper. Roast for 35–40 minutes, or until cooked.

SERVES 8

INGREDIENTS

900 g/2 lb potatoes

55 g/2 oz freshly grated Parmesan

55 g/2 oz dry breadcrumbs

1 egg, lightly beaten

2–3 tbsp extra virgin olive oil

salt and freshly ground black pepper

Roast Potatoes with Breadcrumbs and Parmesan

Be careful not to overcook or the breadcrumbs will taste like burnt toast.

METHOD

Preheat the oven to 220°C/425°F/Gas Mark 7. Cook the potatoes in lightly salted boiling water for about 10 minutes. Drain and shake them dry in the saucepan. Mix the cheese with the breadcrumbs and season to taste. Brush or dip the potatoes in the beaten egg, then in the cheese mixture. Meanwhile, heat the oil in a roasting tin in the preheated oven. Add the potatoes and quickly baste to seal them. Cook for 40 minutes, or until they are tender and golden.

SERVES 6

INGREDIENTS

450–800 g/1 lb
12 oz small new
potatoes
4-6 garlic cloves
115 g/4 oz streaky
bacon, chopped
4 fresh thyme sprigs
4 fresh rosemary
sprigs
3 tbsp olive oil
coarse salt, for
sprinkling

Roast New Potatoes with Bacon, Garlic, Thyme and Rosemary

These are simple to do and full of flavour. If you are using new potatoes, try to get Home Guards, they are the best for this recipe by a long shot. Timing depends on the size of the potatoes and you can, of course, use older potatoes, but don't add the herbs until halfway through the cooking time if you do.

METHOD

Preheat the oven to 220°C/425°F/Gas Mark 7. Place the potatoes, garlic, herbs and bacon in a roasting tin and toss in oil. Roast in the preheated oven for 20–30 minutes, adding the herbs after about 10–15 minutes. Drain and sprinkle with coarse salt.

SERVES 4

INGREDIENTS

900 g/2 lb new
potatoes
2 tbsp butter
2 generous tbsp
chopped fresh mint
2 generous tbsp
snipped fresh chives
salt and freshly
ground black pepper

New Potatoes with Mint and Chives

New potatoes with butter, mint and chives can make you feel that summer has arrived, even if the weather is a bit doubtful. The smell of chopped tender mint leaves and young chives fills the kitchen, and the flavour is hard to beat. If you have never invested in a good, decent-sized steamer, do it now.

METHOD

Scrub the potatoes well, place in a steamer with a good-fitting lid and steam for 15–20 minutes or until tender. Dry off and place in a hot bowl. Melt the butter, remove from the heat, add the herbs and season. Pour over the potatoes and serve at once. These are also good cold.

SERVES 4

INGREDIENTS

6 large potatoes
1 small garlic clove
2-3 tbsp soured
cream or butter
1 tbsp chopped fresh
parsley
1 tbsp snipped fresh
chives
salt and freshly
ground black pepper

Baked Potatoes with Soured Cream, Parsley and Chives

These are a great lunch-time snack on a cold day, or for children just in from school who can't wait for dinner. For the best result, choose good floury potatoes, such as Golden Wonders.

METHOD

Preheat the oven to 220°C/425°F/Gas Mark 7. Scrub the potatoes, prick the tops with a skewer and place on a baking sheet in the preheated oven for 1 hour or until cooked. While they are cooking, peel the garlic and mash it with a little salt until it is smooth. Blend it into the soured cream, add the herbs and season with salt and pepper to taste. Serve as a topping with baked potatoes.

SERVES 6

INGREDIENTS

6 large potatoes
110 g/4 oz white
Cheddar cheese,
grated
2 streaky bacon
rashers, fried and
chopped
1 tbsp cream
1 tbsp butter
salt and freshly
ground black pepper

Baked Potatoes with Cheese and Bacon

This delicious stuffed potato is unexpectedly rich and extremely filling. More than just a snack, they make a good light main course.

METHOD

Preheat the oven to 220°C/425°F/Gas Mark 7. Place the potatoes on a baking sheet and bake them in the preheated oven for 45–60 minutes. When the potatoes are tender, halve them and carefully remove the flesh, making sure to keep the skins intact. Mash the flesh and place in a saucepan with the cheese, bacon, cream and butter. Heat and season carefully – you may not need salt, depending on the bacon. Put the mixture back into the skins, place under a preheated grill for 1 minute and serve.

SERVES 6

INGREDIENTS

900 g/2 lb floury
potatoes
sunflower oil, for
deep-frying
salt and freshly
ground black pepper

Traditional Chips

The trick to a good chip is to use floury
potatoes and make sure the cooking oil is
hot enough – cook in batches, reheating
the oil between batches to ensure this.
Chips must be served immediately.

METHOD

Peel the potatoes and cut lengthways into slices roughly 1.2 cm/
½ inch wide. Soak them in a bowl of salted water for about 10
minutes. Drain and dry thoroughly on a clean tea towel. Heat
the oil to 180°C/350°F, but be careful not to allow it to smoke.
Add the chips and cook for about 7 minutes until beginning to
brown but not crisp. Shake the pan gently, leave to cook for a
further 1–2 minutes, then lift the chips out of the oil. Dry off on
warmed kitchen paper and serve quickly, lightly sprinkled with
salt or pepper.

You can also cook the chips in the hot oil for 5 minutes, lift
them out, dry them on kitchen paper and set them aside for a
while until ready to serve. Heat the oil again and fry the chips
for about 5 minutes, or until they are hot and crisp. Drain in the
usual way.

SERVES 4

INGREDIENTS

900 g/2 lb floury
potatoes, unpeeled
sunflower oil, for
deep-frying
herbes de Provence
salt

Chips with Herbes de Provence

These chips are always a big hit in our
house, as a snack, or with burgers or steak.

METHOD

Scrub the potatoes thoroughly and cook in boiling water for
about 10 minutes. Drain and cut into large chips. Heat the
oil until it is very hot. While the oil is heating, rinse the chips
in cold water and dry thoroughly. Fry the chips for about 5
minutes until they are brown and crispy. Remove them from the
fat and dry them in heated kitchen paper. Sprinkle with herbes
de Provence and salt. Serve immediately.

SERVES 4

INGREDIENTS

675 g/1 lb 8 oz
cooked potatoes
2 tbsp butter
salt and freshly
ground black pepper

Sautéed Potatoes

Sautéed potatoes are a great way of
using up leftover potatoes. Fry them
over a gentle heat rather than at a high
temperature.

METHOD

Slice the cooked potatoes, leaving the skin on if you wish. Heat
the butter in a heavy frying pan, add the potatoes and cook
slowly over a low heat for 15–20 minutes. Turn them at least
once during cooking. The potatoes should be a pale golden
colour and crumbly on all sides. Drain them on warmed kitchen
paper. Season lightly and serve.

For a bit of variation you can add some finely chopped herbs
such as parsley, tarragon (lovely if you are serving them with
chicken) or rosemary.

SERVES 4

INGREDIENTS

900 g/2 lb baby
new potatoes
2 garlic cloves
4 tbsp butter
2 tbsp grated lemon
rind
2 tbsp chopped fresh
parsley
salt

Sautéed Garlic Potatoes

This is a way of jazzing up sautéed
potatoes to make a delicious alternative
with a bit of zest.

METHOD

Scrub and steam the potatoes until they are tender, then drain
and dry off. This can be done in advance and the potatoes can
be kept covered in the fridge until you need them. Peel the
garlic and crush with a little salt until smooth. Heat the butter
in a heavy-based frying pan, add the garlic and potatoes and
cook gently until the potatoes are golden brown. Put them in
a large warmed bowl, add the lemon rind and parsley and toss
carefully. Serve immediately.

SERVES 6

INGREDIENTS

2 potatoes
groundnut oil, for
frying
½ tsp salt
¾ tsp caraway seeds
pinch of cayenne
pepper

Savoury Potato Straws

These make a great snack, but you need to make plenty of them as they will quickly disappear.

METHOD

Peel and grate the potatoes onto a wooden board to allow them to dry. Heat the oil in a frying pan until it spits when you drop in a piece of potato, then add the potato and fry until golden brown. Drain well on warmed kitchen paper. Combine the salt, caraway seeds and cayenne pepper and sprinkle over the potatoes. These can be eaten hot or cold.

SERVES 4

Potato Sticks

These are quicker to make than they sound and are popular served on their own as something to nibble.

INGREDIENTS

170 g/6 oz floury potatoes

175 g/6 oz butter

175 g/6 oz plain flour, plus extra for dusting

1 egg yolk

2 tbsp top-of-the-bottle full-cream milk

poppy seeds, coarse sea salt and caraway seeds, for sprinkling

salt and freshly ground black pepper

METHOD

Preheat the oven to 200°C/400°F/Gas Mark 6. Lightly dust a baking sheet with flour. Cook the potatoes in lightly salted boiling water until almost tender. Drain and leave to cool. Grate the potatoes coarsely, mix with the butter and flour and season well with salt and pepper.

Knead to a smooth dough and divide into four sections. Make a long roll with each section and cut into 16 finger-length pieces; score them across the top with a knife. Beat the egg yolk with the cream and brush the fingers with the mixture.

Place on the prepared baking sheet, then sprinkle one-third of the fingers with caraway seeds, one-third with poppy seeds and the remainder with coarse sea salt. Bake in the preheated oven for 10–12 minutes.

SERVES 4

MAIN COURSES

We don't often think of potatoes as a main dish, but why not? And for protein, just add cheese, eggs, fish or meat. Easy!

Bíodh práta dhá ithe agus práta dhá scú agat,
dgá práta ud gcúl do dhoirn agus do shúil ar dhá
ohráta ar on mbord!
Be eating a potato, peeling a potato, have two in
your hand and an eye on two more on the table!

Irish Saying

INGREDIENTS

8 large eggs, beaten

100 g/3½ oz cottage cheese

125 g/4½ oz wafer-thin smoked ham, roughly torn

1 tbsp olive oil

1 onion, finely chopped

2 potatoes, thinly sliced

salt and freshly ground black pepper

green salad, to serve

Oven-Baked Potato and Ham Frittata

This is very easy to prepare, and you don't need to worry about it getting singed under the grill. Don't be tempted to use cooked potatoes – they won't work.

METHOD

Preheat the oven to 180°C/350°F/Gas Mark 4. Combine the eggs, cheese and ham in a large bowl and season to taste with salt and pepper.

Pour the oil into an ovenproof frying pan, add the onion and fry over a medium heat until translucent. Add the potato slices in a single layer, then pour in the egg mixture and cook, without stirring, for 5 minutes until the base of the frittata is set.

Transfer to the preheated oven and cook for 25–30 minutes until the egg is cooked and the top is golden. Cover with a piece of kitchen foil if it is browning too quickly. Serve hot with a green salad.

SERVES 4

INGREDIENTS

1 tbsp butter, plus extra for greasing

1 leek, roughly chopped

½ tsp fresh thyme

250 ml/9 fl oz crème fraîche

¼ tsp chopped dried chilli

pinch of freshly grated nutmeg

450 g/1 lb butternut squash, thinly sliced

225 g/8 oz potatoes, thinly sliced

55 g/2 oz Cheddar cheese, grated

salt and freshly ground black pepper

Butternut Squash and Potato Gratin

The lovely autumn flavours of butternut squash combine well with potatoes in this delicious accompaniment to roast chicken or meat.

METHOD

Preheat the oven to 200°C/400°F/Gas Mark 6. Grease a baking dish with butter. Melt the butter in a heavy-based saucepan, add the leek, season with salt and pepper and leave to sweat for 5 minutes. Remove from the heat and add the thyme. Place the crème fraîche, chilli and nutmeg in a saucepan, heat gently, then remove from the heat and keep warm.

Mix the squash and potatoes together and place a layer on the base of the prepared dish, followed by half of the leeks. Pour over a third of the liquid, followed by another layer of potatoes and squash and then the remaining leeks. Pour over a little more liquid, layer the remaining potatoes and cover with the remaining liquid. Sprinkle the cheese on top and bake in the preheated oven for 30–35 minutes until golden.

SERVES 4

INGREDIENTS

2 tbsp olive oil
1 onion, finely chopped
5–6 large ripe tomatoes, peeled and chopped
500 g/1 lb 2 oz hot mashed potatoes
3 egg yolks
150 ml/5 fl oz cream
55 g/2 oz butter
chopped fresh oregano, to taste
salt and freshly ground black pepper
freshly grated Parmesan cheese, to garnish

Mashed Potatoes with Tomato and Parmesan

This is a big dish, really tasty and filling. The tomatoes in the middle are great on their own as a sauce or on toast.

METHOD

Heat the oil in a frying pan, and the onion and tomatoes, cook gently and season well. Put the potatoes into a bowl, then beat in the egg yolks, cream and butter until well blended. Add the oregano and season well. Arrange the potatoes around the edge of a serving dish, then and put the tomatoes in the middle and sprinkle with cheese. Serve immediately.

SERVES 4

INGREDIENTS

1 large butternut
squash, peeled and
cut lengthways into
6 pieces

1½ tbsp sunflower
oil, plus extra for
brushing

150 g/5 oz chopped
onion

2 heaped dsp yellow
curry paste

800 ml/1½ pints
coconut milk

200 ml/7 fl oz water

4 kaffir lime leaves

3 tsp Madras curry
powder

1 tsp turmeric

1 tsp salt

20 g/1 oz or 1 dsp
palm sugar

300 g/10½ oz
potatoes, diced and
parboiled

cooked jasmine rice,
to serve

SERVES 4

Roasted Butternut Squash and Potato Curry

Tao in Saba Restaurant in Dublin gave me this from his wonderful book *SABA: The Cookbook.* Like everything Tao cooks, it is really tasty and delicious as well as being quick and easy to make.

METHOD

Preheat the oven to 180°C/350°F/Gas Mark 4.

Brush the squash with a little oil, place in a heavy roasting tin and bake in the preheated oven for about 30 minutes until it begins to soften. Remove from the oven and set aside.

Heat a wok over a medium heat, add the oil, chopped onion and curry paste and stir until it begins to release an aroma. Add the coconut milk and water, bring to the boil, then add the kaffir lime leaves, curry powder and turmeric with the salt and sugar, and stir until the sugar has dissolved. Add the potatoes and squash and cook for about three minutes. Serve immediately with rice.

INGREDIENTS

350 g/12 oz cooking apples, peeled and cored
25 g/1 oz sugar
knob of butter
650 g/1 lb 7 oz mashed potatoes
1 tbsp sunflower oil
350 g/12 oz black pudding
1 onion, chopped
salt and freshly ground black pepper
chopped fresh parsley and finely chopped spring onions, to garnish

Potatoes with Apple and Black Pudding

We have the best black pudding here in Ireland. I am a big fan of Inch and Jack McCarthy's pudding but there are lots available and many butchers are making their own, always worth trying. This is a hearty dish.

METHOD

Cook the apples with a little water until soft. Add the sugar and butter and beat well. Add to the mashed potatoes and season well. Heat the oil in a heavy frying pan, add the black pudding and cook quickly on both sides (don't overcook it). Remove from the pan, add the onions and fry gently until just beginning to turn golden.

Put the black pudding on a warmed serving dish with the potatoes in the centre, sprinkle with parsley and spring onions and serve.

SERVES 4

INGREDIENTS

55 g/2 oz butter,
plus extra for
greasing
1 onion, finely
chopped
600 g/1 lb 5 oz hot
mashed potatoes
1 free-range egg,
beaten
150 g/5½ oz butter
150 g/5½ oz
Cheddar cheese,
grated
½ tsp Dijon mustard
large bunch of
snipped fresh chives
salt and freshly
ground black pepper

Baked Mashed Potato

This delicious dish is a cross between a potato dauphinoise and a rösti. Delicious served both warm and cold, it is great for taking on a picnic.

METHOD

Preheat the oven to 200°C/400°F/Gas Mark 6. Grease a 23-cm/9-inch springform cake tin or an oven-proof dish with butter. Melt half the butter in a heavy based saucepan, add the onion, cover and leave to sweat gently until transparent.

Combine all the ingredients and mix well. Spread the mixture evenly in the prepared tin or dish and dot the top with the remaining butter. Bake in the preheated oven for 25 minutes or until golden. Cut into wedges to serve.

SERVES 4

INGREDIENTS

butter, for greasing
125 ml/4 fl oz chicken or vegetable stock
150 ml/5 fl oz cream
150 ml/5 fl oz milk
1 large garlic clove, crushed
1 bay leaf
700 g/1 lb 9 oz potatoes, peeled and sliced
2 leeks, thinly sliced
100 g/3½ oz Cheddar cheese, grated
salt and freshly ground black pepper

Potato, Leek and Cheese Pie

Perfect as a main dish or served with a good side of ham and it is quick to prepare. Use a mandolin to slice the potatoes and leeks.

METHOD

Preheat the oven to 180°C/350°F/Gas Mark 4. Grease a 2-litre/3½-pint baking dish with butter. Put the stock, cream and milk into a small saucepan with the garlic and bay leaf and bring to the boil. Remove from the heat, cover and set aside.

Mix the potatoes and leeks together and spread them in the prepared dish in an even layer. Pour over the liquid with the bay leaf and season well. Cover with the grated cheese.

Place a piece of kitchen foil over the top of the dish and place in the oven for 1 hour or until cooked. Halfway through the cooking time, remove the foil so that the top will be crisp and golden, but take care that it doesn't burn.

SERVES 4

INGREDIENTS

1.5 kg/3 lb 5 oz
peeled potatoes
sunflower oil, for
frying
1 tsp black mustard
seeds
1 tsp cumin seeds
1 onion, diced
2 red chillies,
deseeded and finely
chopped
¼ tsp turmeric
1 tsp lemon juice
1 tsp dried coriander
1 tsp curry powder
1 tbsp chopped fresh
coriander
30 g/1 oz cooked
garden peas
12 sheets filo pastry
225 g/8 oz natural
yogurt
1 tsp finely chopped
fresh mint
salt

MAKES 12

Potato Samosas

This is one of the addictive, delicious recipes from the talented Pamela and Lorraine in Blazing Salads in Dublin.

METHOD

Bring a large saucepan of lightly salted water to the boil, add the potatoes, bring back to the boil and simmer until the potatoes are tender but not mushy. Drain and set aside to cool.

Pour a little oil into a small saucepan and place over a medium heat. Add the black mustard seeds and cumin seeds and heat until popping. Add the onion and chillies and sauté until the onion is soft. Remove from the heat. Chop the potatoes roughly. Add the onion, chillies, seeds, turmeric, lemon juice, dried coriander and curry powder and mix together. Season with salt. Stir in the fresh coriander and the peas.

Unwrap the filo pastry sheets. Take 1 sheet and spread it out flat. Fold into three lengthways. Repeat with all the sheets. Divide the filling into 12 portions. Take one of the folded sheets and place it widthways in front of you. Place a portion of the filling at the bottom lefthand corner of the pastry. Fold over into a triangle. Continue folding until all the pastry is used. Repeat with remaining filling and pastry.

Heat enough oil in a saucepan for deep frying. Drop the samosas into the hot oil and cook until golden. Remove and drain on kitchen paper. Place the yogurt in a bowl and add the fresh mint and a little salt. Serve with the samosas.

INGREDIENTS

200 g/7 oz onions, thinly sliced

4 tbsp olive oil

225 g/8 oz plum tomatoes, peeled and chopped

1 tsp dried or freshly chopped oregano

1 tsp sugar (optional)

500 g/1 lb 2 oz new potatoes, peeled and cut into cubes

fresh oregano, to garnish

salt and freshly ground black pepper

New Potatoes with Tomatoes and Onions

This lovely mixture of onions, potatoes and fresh tomatoes is delicious with fish and chicken dishes, or can be served as a hearty lunch dish.

METHOD

Place the onions in a heavy-based saucepan with the oil and cook gently until they begin to colour. Add the tomatoes and oregano, and season well. Taste – you may need to add a little sugar. Cook over a low heat for about 15 minutes. Add the potatoes, cover the pan and leave to cook slowly for a further 20 minutes or until the potatoes are cooked.

Serve hot or cold.

SERVES 4

INGREDIENTS

900 g/2 lb neck end
or gigot chops of
lamb, cut into thick
pieces
3 onions, sliced
4-6 potatoes, peeled
and quartered
600 ml/1 pint brown
stock or water
salt and freshly
ground black pepper
chopped fresh
parsley, to garnish

Irish Stew

A very traditional and nutritious Irish recipe. Add carrots if you wish.

METHOD

Put a layer of lamb in the base of a heavy casserole dish. Follow with a layer of onions, salt and pepper and a layer of potatoes. Repeat until all the ingredients are used up, finishing with potatoes. Add the stock and bring to the boil. Simmer gently for about 1½ hours. It is best not to let it cook too quickly: watch it carefully.

Irish Stew is greasy so if you have time, drain off the liquid, leave to cool and skim off the fat. Return the liquid to the casserole and bring to the boil. Remove any bones, using a fork. Replace the liquid and heat it again. Sprinkle with parsley and serve hot.

SERVES 6

INGREDIENTS

350 g/12 oz
potatoes

225 g/8 oz cooked
fish, such as cod or
salmon

55 g/2 oz butter,
melted

1 egg, beaten

2 tbsp chives, finely
chopped

55 g/2 oz dry
breadcrumbs

salt and freshly
ground black pepper

Fish Cakes

Handy, economical and tasty, you can use
most fish for this basic recipe. Vary the
proportion of potato to fish to suit your
taste and use whatever fresh herbs you
have to hand – parsley, chives, fennel or a
clove of garlic, crushed.

METHOD

Cook and mash the potatoes. Remove the bones or skin from
the fish and add to the mashed potato. Add melted butter and
a *little* beaten egg to bind the mixture. It needs only a little egg,
otherwise it will be runny and difficult to cook. Season with salt
and pepper and mix in the chives. Divide the mixture into little
flat cakes. Dip in the beaten egg and then in the breadcrumbs
to coat. Heat the oil in a frying pan, then add the fish cakes and
cook for 1–2 minutes on each side. They should be golden and
crisp on both sides.

SERVES 4

INGREDIENTS

1 litre/1¾ pints
water
8 thick slices ham or
bacon, chopped
8 large pork
sausages, cut into
large chunks
4 large onions,
peeled and sliced
900 g/2 lb potatoes,
peeled and sliced
4 tbsp chopped fresh
parsley
salt and freshly
ground black pepper

Dublin Coddle

Coddle is tasty and simple to make but doesn't appeal to everyone. A traditional dish that fell out of favour in recent years, it has begun to reappear on smart restaurant menus. Serve in warmed bowls with a glass of Guinness stout or ale and brown bread.

METHOD

Bring the water to the boil and drop in the ham and sausages. Cook for 5 minutes, drain and reserve the water. Place the ham and sausages in a large saucepan or casserole dish, add the onions, potatoes and half the parsley and season with salt and pepper. Add enough of the reserved liquid to just cover. Place greased paper on top, cover with a lid and then simmer gently for about 1½ hours, until the liquid has reduced and everything is cooked. Serve in warmed bowls.

SERVES 4–6

INGREDIENTS

2 tbsp butter
1 onion, chopped
2 carrots, sliced
4 tbsp flour
600 ml/1 pint brown stock
chopped fresh parsley and thyme
450 g/1 lb cooked minced beef or lamb
675 g/1 lb 8 oz mashed potatoes
55 g/2 oz Cheddar cheese, grated

Shepherd's Pie

This is usually made with beef left over from the Sunday joint, or any other meat. It tastes quite different when raw beef is used, and many would argue that, made from raw beef, it is not Shepherd's Pie at all but Cottage Pie.

METHOD

Preheat the oven to 180°C/350°F/Gas Mark 4. Melt the butter in a saucepan and add the onion. Cover and leave to sweat for a few minutes. Add the carrots. Stir in the flour and cook until it is slightly browned. Add the stock and herbs, bring to the boil and boil for 5 minutes until the the liquid is slightly reduced. Add the meat and bring it back to the boil. Place in a pie dish and cover with the mashed potatoes.

Bake in the preheated oven for about 30 minutes. Sprinkle the cheese over the potatoes 10 minutes before the end of the cooking time.

SERVES 4

INGREDIENTS

1 pre-rolled short
crust pastry case

4-6 organic Irish
potatoes (skins on)

1 medium onion

2 cloves roasted
garlic

200g free range
smoked bacon
lardons

Salt & pepper

Olive oil

Sprig of rosemary &
thyme

3 tablespoons crème
fraîche

6 slices of Durrus
cheese or a wash
rind cheese

Irish Style Tartiflette

Another delicious recipe from the fabulous
Pepper Pot Café in Powerscourt Townhouse
in Dublin.

Method

Preheat the oven to 200° C/400° F/Gas Mark 6. Take the pre-oiled
pastry case, line it with greaseproof paper and fill with porcelain
baking beans to weigh down the pastry and prevent it from rising
in the oven. Remove after 15 minutes or when lightly golden.

Wash and dry the potoatoes and very thinly slice along the onion
and roasted cloves of garlic with a mandolin. Place in a baking dish
drizzle with olive oil, salt and pepper. Add the lardons and sprig of
herbs and mix gently.

Cover with a lid or with tin foil and bake in the oven for 15–20
minutes. Remove the lid and continue to bake, stirring every so
often to allow the onions to caramelise. Once the potatoes are
cooked thoroughly and the mix is slightly charred and sticky,
remove from the oven adding the crème fraîche and stir rapidly.
The juices combine and create a wonderful creamy smoky sauce.

Remove beans and paper from the pastry case.

Fill the case with the delicious deconstructed gratin-like mixture.
Layer with Durrus cheese. Bake for 10 minutes or so.

Serve with dressed organic leaves and homemade red onion
marmalade.

SERVES 6

INGREDIENTS

675 g/1 lb 8 oz cod
2 hard-boiled eggs, finely chopped
1 heaped tbsp chopped parsley and capers, mixed
2 tbsp butter
4 tbsp plain flour
1 litre/1¾ pints hot fish stock
1 glass white wine
450 g/1 lb potatoes, boiled and mashed
salt and freshly ground black pepper

Fish Pie

Use cod or any white fish to make this deliciously rich pie. It's easy to make so adapt it to your own tastes using more or less fish or some vegetables, and do use good fish stock.

METHOD

Poach the fish for about 5 minutes, then remove from the water. Remove any small bones from the fish, break it up gently and place in a large baking dish. Add the eggs and sprinkle with the herb and caper mixture. Melt the butter in a small saucepan, stir in the flour carefully and add the warm stock and wine. Bring to the boil and cook for about 20 minutes, allowing the stock to reduce by about half. Season and pour over the fish.

Meanwhile, preheat the oven to 180°C/350°F/Gas Mark 4. Add the stock to the mashed potatoes and spread over the fish. Cook in the preheated oven for 25 minutes, or until the potatoes are golden brown.

SERVES 6

INGREDIENTS

800 g/1 lb 12 oz
white fish, such as
cod or coley, and
some prawns or
salmon for style
200 ml/7 fl oz milk
2 hard-boiled eggs
2 tsp capers
800 g/1 lb 12 oz hot
mashed potatoes
peas or petits pois,
to serve

White Sauce

15 g/½ oz butter
15 g/½ oz plain
flour
300 ml/10 fl oz milk
salt and freshly
ground black pepper

Jean's Fish Pie

This is an old family favourite in the
publisher's house, with everyone divided
as to whether they like the capers or not.
You could add capers separately at one
end of the dish only, and make a pattern
in the potato with a fork so that you
remember which end is which.

METHOD

Preheat the oven to 180°C/350°F/Gas Mark 4. To make the white
sauce, melt the butter in a small saucepan, stir in the flour and
cook for 1–2 minutes. Remove from the heat and gradually stir
the milk to make a smooth sauce. Return to the heat, bring to th
boil and simmer gently for 10 minutes. Season to taste.

Poach the fish in the milk for about 7 minutes until the flesh is
opaque. Line an ovenproof dish with the fish, broken into piece
to fill the base. Cut the eggs into quarters and spread them over
the fish. Add the capers to the white sauce to taste – use as man
or as few as you like. Pour the white sauce over the fish so that
is completely covered. Carefully spoon the mashed potato over
the white sauce and flatten the surface with the back of a fork.

Bake in the preheated oven for 20 minutes or until the potato is
a nice golden brown. Serve with peas.

SERVES 4

INGREDIENTS

1 kg/2 lb small new potatoes
3 tbsp olive oil
3 tbsp butter
2-3 anchovies
2 garlic cloves, crushed with a little salt
2 tbsp chopped fresh parsley
150 ml/5 fl oz water
2 tbsp lemon juice
salt and freshly ground black pepper

Baked New Potatoes with Anchovies and Parsley

This recipe is a really good lunch dish served with crusty bread and, yes, a salad of green leaves.

METHOD

Preheat the oven to 200°C/400°F/Gas Mark 6. Scrub the potatoes and pat dry. Heat the oil and butter in a heavy-based roasting tin set over a medium heat. Add the anchovy fillets and cook for 1 minute, mashing the anchovy fillets into the oil with a fork. Add the potatoes and fry for a few minutes until they are beginning to colour. Add the garlic, parsley and water, followed by the lemon juice and salt and pepper to taste.

Bake in the preheated oven for about 20 minutes, basting once. Serve in a warmed dish and pour over the juice from the tin.

SERVES 4

INGREDIENTS

225 g/8 oz new potatoes

good bunch of asparagus

6 eggs

55–85 g/2–3 oz freshly grated Parmesan cheese

225 g/8 oz fresh or frozen broad beans, cooked and skinned

3 tbsp chopped herbs, such as parsley, thyme or tarragon

4 tbsp butter

salt and freshly ground black pepper

Potatoes with Asparagus, Beans and Parmesan

This dish makes a very rich and filling main course, but it's important to use good cheese.

METHOD

Steam the potatoes until just cooked. Leave to cool, then cut into thick slices. Trim the asparagus and steam for 12 minutes before dipping into cold water quickly. Drain and cut into short lengths.

Put the eggs in a bowl with salt and pepper to taste and half the cheese. Beat until well blended, then stir in the beans, asparagus and herbs. Melt half the butter in a heavy-based frying pan. When it foams, add the egg mixture and reduce the heat. Leave to cook very slowly for 10–15 minutes, or until set on the bottom but with the top still a bit runny.

Arrange the sliced potatoes over the top, sprinkle with the remaining cheese and dot with the remaining butter. Place under a very hot grill until the top begins to brown. Do not take your eye off it at this point or it will become dry and leathery. Cut into thick wedges and serve at once.

SERVES 4

INGREDIENTS

700 g/1 lb 8 oz
small new potatoes
2 tbsp olive oil
225 g/8 oz onions
1 garlic clove, finely
chopped
2 tsp paprika
2 tsp plain flour
2 tbsp red wine
vinegar
150–300 ml/
5–10 fl oz white
stock
1 green pepper,
blanched and
chopped
2 tomatoes, peeled
and deseeded
salt and freshly
ground black pepper
2 tbsp yogurt or
soured cream, to
garnish

Potato Casserole

It is important to blanch the green pepper for this recipe or it will be too strong, so if you are going to take a shortcut, choose some other one.

METHOD

Cook the potatoes in boiling water for 15 minutes. Heat the oil in a heavy casserole dish, add the onions and garlic and cook until golden but not brown. Stir in the paprika and cook for a further minute. Remove from the heat and blend in the flour, vinegar and enough stock to thicken the liquid. Season with salt and pepper and bring to the boil. Drain the potatoes and add to the casserole with the green pepper and tomatoes. Cook for a further 5–10 minutes until the potatoes are tender. Just before serving, spoon in the yogurt and stir gently.

SERVES 4

INGREDIENTS

900 g/2 lb floury
potatoes
450 g/1 lb Italian
pork sausages
6 tbsp butter, plus
extra for greasing
2 tbsp chopped fresh
parsley
300 ml/10 fl oz
milk, warmed
freshly grated
nutmeg, to taste
2 egg yolks, beaten
2 tbsp freshly grated
Parmesan cheese
salt and freshly
ground black pepper

Sausage and Potato Pie

This is a real winter pie which we all love
and which is very tasty and quick to make.

METHOD

Preheat the oven to 190°C/375°F/Gas Mark 5. Grease a baking
dish with butter. Cook the potatoes in lightly salted boiling
water until tender. Meanwhile, skin the sausages, break up
the meat with a fork, add to the frying pan and fry until lightly
browned. Drain the potatoes, peel, mash well and add the
butter and parsley. Add the sausage meat, milk, nutmeg, egg
yolks and cheese and season to taste with salt and pepper. Beat
well with a wooden spoon. Put the mixture into the prepared
dish and bake in the preheated oven for 30 minutes or until the
top is brown.

SERVES 4

INGREDIENTS

1–2 potatoes, peeled and diced

few sprigs of fresh rosemary, finely chopped

4 eggs

1½ tbsp cold water

2 tbsp butter, plus extra for frying

salt and freshly ground black pepper

Potato Omelette

Omelettes are so versatile and so easy to prepare, and you will find one for every occasion. The potatoes make a hearty meal of this one, perfect for lunch or a light supper. Do not add the potatoes to the omelette until the last minute.

METHOD

You can use raw or left-over potatoes for this. Melt some butter in a frying pan, add the potatoes and fry, adding the rosemary just before the potato is cooked.

Break the eggs into a bowl and beat well with a fork. Add the water and season. Put the butter into a frying pan, and when it begins to froth, add the egg mixture. Leave to cook for about 15 seconds before stirring it with the back of a fork, drawing up the cooked egg to allow the raw egg to cook. Do this a couple of times until the omelette is just cooked. Put the potato mixture in the middle, fold the omelette over and serve at once.

SERVES 2–3

INGREDIENTS

900 g/2 lb floury potatoes, such as Queens

225 g/8 oz plain flour, plus extra for dusting

4 tbsp butter, melted

55 g/2 oz freshly grated Parmesan cheese

salt and freshly ground black pepper

Roman Gnocchi

It is traditional to serve Gnocchi alla Romana on Thursdays in Roman trattorie.

METHOD

Cook the potatoes in lightly salted boiling water until tender. Drain well and dry them thoroughly – it is important to get them as dry as possible. Mash until smooth, put them in a mixing bowl and add salt and pepper. Then add the flour, little by little, to make a good firm dough. Knead the dough for 1–2 minutes, then divide it into 4 equal-sized pieces. Roll out each piece into a cylinder shape about 1.2 cm/½ inch thick, cut into 2.5-cm/1-inch pieces and pinch in the middle. Dust lightly with flour.

Preheat the oven to 200°C/400°F/Gas Mark 6. Bring a large saucepan of lightly salted water to the boil and drop in as many of the gnocchi as will comfortably fit. Boil rapidly until they rise to the surface. Lift them out, drain thoroughly and place in a warmed dish. Pour over the melted butter and cover generously with cheese. Place them in the preheated oven for a couple of minutes until the cheese has melted slightly, then serve.

SERVES 6 AS A STARTER, 4 AS A MAIN COURSE

INGREDIENTS

Pizza base

675 g/1 lb 8 oz
floury potatoes

4–5 tbsp olive
oil, plus extra for
brushing

plain flour, for
dusting

salt and freshly
ground black pepper

Topping

450 g/1 lb tomatoes

chopped oregano or
parsley

175 g/6 oz
mozzarella cheese

55 g/2 oz freshly
grated Parmesan
cheese

12 black olives,
stoned and
quartered

olive oil, for drizzling

salt and freshly
ground black pepper

SERVES 4

Potato Pizza with Mozzarella

If you have a pizza oven or cook in a stove
such as an Aga or Stanley, put the baking
sheet on the floor of the oven so that the
base will be really crispy. You can use both
parsley and oregano together.

METHOD

Preheat the oven to 190°C/375°F/Gas Mark 5. To make the
base, wash the potatoes and boil them in their jackets until
tender. Drain well, cool, peel and mash until they are quite
smooth. Add enough oil to make a smooth mixture, then add
salt and pepper to taste. Lightly brush a baking sheet with oil
and sprinkle with flour. Spread the potato dough on the baking
sheet in a large even round.

To make the topping, peel the tomatoes, liquidise them with
oregano or parsley and spread on top of the base. Season well.
Slice the mozzarella cheese finely, cut each slice in half and lay
on top of the tomatoes, followed by the Parmesan cheese and
the olives. Drizzle a little oil on top and bake in the preheated
oven for 15–20 minutes, or until the cheese is melting and just
beginning to brown.

SIDE DISHES AND ACCOMPANIMENTS

You could serve most of these dishes as an accompaniment to a meat, fish or vegetarian main course, but some make a great main course in themselves, served with green vegetables or a fresh salad.

Plúr an phráta a theas.
The floury part of the potato is the hottest.

Irish Saying

INGREDIENTS

1 kg/2 lb 4 oz small
new potatoes, such
as Home Guard

15 g/½ oz butter

1 small fennel bulb,
finely chopped

2 heaped tbsp finely
chopped mint

salt and freshly
ground black pepper

New Potatoes with Fennel and Mint

Love or hate fennel? It seems there is nothing in between so this is for the fennel lovers.

METHOD

Steam the potatoes or cook them in a saucepan of boiling water until just tender.

Melt the butter in a heavy-based frying pan, add the fennel and gently cook until it is just beginning to brown. Remove from the heat and season to taste with salt and pepper.

Add the potatoes and mint and toss well so that the potatoes are coated in the butter. Check the seasoning and serve warm.

SERVES 4

INGREDIENTS

500 g/1 lb 2 oz
potatoes
1 large onion
250 g/9 oz small
parsnips
25 g/1 oz butter
¼ tsp freshly ground
nutmeg
150 ml/5 fl oz milk
150 ml/5 fl oz
cream or crème
fraîche
salt and freshly
ground black pepper

Potatoes with Parsnips and Onions

This rich and luxurious side dish is the perfect accompaniment to the Sunday roast or the Christmas turkey or goose.

METHOD

Preheat the oven to 180°C/350°F/Gas Mark 4. Grease a large ovenproof dish.

Slice the potatoes, parsnips and onions into 5-mm/¼-inch rings and layer the rings in the prepared dish. Dot a little butter on the potato layers, and season each layer with salt and pepper and the nutmeg. Finish with a layer of potatoes and pour over the milk and cream.

Cover with kitchen foil and bake in the preheated oven for 1½–2 hours. Remove the foil for the last 20 minutes of cooking to brown the potatoes.

SERVES 4

INGREDIENTS

500 g/1 lb 2 oz new
potatoes

3 tbsp olive oil

225 g/8 oz
tomatoes, chopped

3 fresh bay leaves,
torn

salt and freshly
ground black pepper

Cypriot Potatoes

This is a fresh-tasting dish that goes very
well with fish and chicken dishes. It's also
delicious served cold with cold meat.

METHOD

Preheat the oven to 180°C/350°F/Gas Mark 4.

Cook the potatoes in boiling water for 10–15 minutes. Slit each
one with a knife and place in a baking dish with the oil and salt
and pepper to taste. Add the tomatoes and bay leaves and mix
together. Bake in the preheated oven for 40 minutes.

SERVES 4

INGREDIENTS

55 g/2 oz butter

1 large onion, chopped

450 g/1 lb beetroot, peeled and grated

1 large cooking apple, peeled and grated

400 g/14 oz potatoes, peeled and diced

2 tbsp white wine vinegar

1 tsp sugar

salt and freshly ground black pepper

Potatoes and Beetroot

This is far nicer than it sounds! The apple and beetroot go surprisingly well with the potatoes and onions.

METHOD

Melt the butter in a heavy-based saucepan, add the onion and sweat. Add the beetroot, apple and potatoes and toss, ensuring they are well coated with the butter. Add the vinegar and sugar. Cover the pan and cook over a low heat for about 20 minutes, giving the pan a shake occasionally to prevent anything sticking. Serve immediately.

SERVES 4

Ingredients

butter, for greasing

50 ml/2 fl oz crème fraîche

150 ml/5 fl oz cream

1 garlic clove, peeled

2 fresh rosemary sprigs

400 g/14 oz fresh young spinach or 250 g/9 oz frozen leaf spinach, thawed

pinch of freshly grated nutmeg

800 g/1 lb 12 oz sweet potato, well scrubbed and thinly sliced

30 g/1 oz freshly grated Parmesan cheese

salt and freshly ground black pepper

Sweet Potato with Spinach

Great as an accompaniment to lamb or as a main course. Be generous with the spinach.

METHOD

Preheat the oven to 200°C/400°F/Gas Mark 6. Grease an ovenproof dish with butter. Heat the crème fraîche and cream in a saucepan along with the garlic and the rosemary, but do not allow to boil. Add salt and pepper and set aside.

Wash and strain the spinach, place in a colander and wilt it slightly by pouring boiling water over it and draining well. Season with salt and pepper and a pinch of nutmeg.

Spread half the sweet potato over the base of the prepared dish, then add a layer of spinach and finish with the remaining potatoes. Strain the crème fraîche to remove the garlic and rosemary, pour it over the potatoes and top with the grated cheese.

Place a piece of kitchen foil on top and bake in the preheated oven for about 40 minutes. Remove the foil and cook for a further 10 minutes.

SERVES 4

INGREDIENTS

800 g/1 lb 12 oz potatoes

2–3 garlic cloves, chopped

2–3 tbsp extra virgin olive oil

3 tbsp soured cream

3 tsp pesto

1 tbsp chopped fresh basil

salt and freshly ground black pepper

Mashed Potatoes with Basil and Soured Cream

These luxurious mashed potatoes are very easy to prepare. You can peel the potatoes before cooking them, if you prefer.

METHOD

Bring the potatoes to the boil in a saucepan of water and cook until tender. Peel them and leave to dry off.

Return the potatoes to a dry saucepan and mash well. Add the oil, soured cream, garlic, pesto and season. Add the fresh basil and serve.

SERVES 4

INGREDIENTS

1 head of celeriac
500 g/1 lb 2 oz
potatoes
10 g/¼ oz butter
a little hot milk
salt and freshly
ground black pepper

Purée of Celeriac and Potato

Celeriac looks very unpromising, but its unusual flavour combines perfectly with mashed potato to make the ultimate winter side dish.

METHOD

Peel the celeriac and cut into cubes. Peel the potatoes and boil them with the celeriac until tender. Drain well and leave to steam off. Mash well with the butter and salt and pepper to taste. Beat well, adding a little hot milk, until light and fluffy.

SERVES 4

INGREDIENTS

900 g/2 lb potatoes, peeled

2 tbsp semolina

4 tbsp olive oil

salt and freshly ground black pepper

Crispy Roast Potatoes

This is the oldest trick in the book to get really crispy, light roast potatoes – a good hot oven and semolina.

METHOD

Preheat the oven to 230°C/450°F/Gas Mark 8. Put the peeled potatoes in a saucepan of cold water and bring to the boil. Boil for about 5 minutes, drain very well, then place the pan over the heat for a few minutes so that the potatoes dry out. Add the semolina, cover and shake very well so that it spreads evenly and so the potatoes get a rough surface on the outside.

Heat the oil in a heavy roasting tin, then add the potatoes and season with salt and pepper.

Cook in the preheated oven for about 40 minutes, giving the tin a good shake at regular intervals to prevent the potatoes sticking. Serve straight from the oven.

SERVES 4

INGREDIENTS

3 tbsp olive oil

2 beetroots, peeled and cut into 4-cm/1½-inch pieces

250 g/9 oz small potatoes, scrubbed

2 streaky bacon rashers, chopped

200 g/7 oz crème fraîche

½ garlic clove, crushed

2 tsp Dijon mustard

100 g/3½ oz rocket

Roast Potatoes and Beetroot with Crème Fraîche and Mustard

This unlikely collection of ingredients combines to make a deliciously creamy side dish with a very unusual appearance.

METHOD

Preheat the oven to 200°C/400°F/Gas Mark 6. Pour the oil into a heavy roasting tin, then place in the preheated oven for a few minutes until hot. Add the beetroot and potatoes and toss to ensure they are well coated. Return to the oven and roast for about 30 minutes, tossing occasionally. Add the bacon and cook for a further 10 minutes until the rashers are cooked.

Combine the crème fraîche, garlic and mustard in a small bowl. Toss the rocket into the roast beetroot and potatoes and serve with the crème fraîche mixture.

SERVES 4

INGREDIENTS

4 tbsp olive oil

900 g/2 lb floury potatoes, peeled and halved

1 garlic bulb, broken into individual cloves, unpeeled

2 handfuls of fresh sage

salt and freshly ground black pepper

Roast Potatoes with Garlic and Sage

These are delicious, but you need to watch that the sage leaves don't burn.

METHOD

Preheat the oven to 200°C/400°F/Gas Mark 6. Pour the oil into a heavy roasting tin, then place in the preheated oven for a few minutes until hot. Place the potatoes in the tin, turning to coat in the oil, then roast for 15 minutes, shaking the tin occasionally to make sure the potatoes don't stick. Add the garlic cloves and roast for a further 15 minutes. Add the whole sage leaves, making sure that they are coated with oil and roast for a further 5–10 minutes – the leaves should be crisp and not burnt. Lightly season with salt and pepper and serve immediately.

SERVES 4

INGREDIENTS

¾ tbsp vegetable oil
900 g/2 lb sweet
potatoes, cubed
pinch of cumin seeds
pinch of dried red
chillies
salt and freshly
ground pepper

Simple Roast Sweet Potatoes

This is one of the nicest ways to prepare
sweet potatoes. The roasting method
brings out all their sweet flavour. Cooking
time will depend on the size of the sweet
potato cubes – don't let them get mushy.

METHOD

Preheat the oven to 200°C/400°F/Gas Mark 6. Pour the oil into
a heavy roasting tin, then place in the preheated oven for a
few minutes until hot. Scrub the potatoes well. Season with
the cumin seeds, chillies and salt and pepper and roast for 15
minutes, or until tender.

SERVES 4

INGREDIENTS

juice of 1 small lemon

6 tbsp extra virgin olive oil

a few sun-dried tomatoes, roughly chopped

10–15 whole black olives, stoned

1 tbsp juicy capers, roughly chopped

½ small red onion, finely chopped

1 garlic clove, very finely chopped (optional)

fresh herbs of your choice, to taste

750 g/1 lb 10 oz small waxy new potatoes

salt

Farmgate Café Black Olive and Sun-Dried Tomato Crushed Potatoes

Nobody can say they have experienced The English Market in Cork without a visit to the Farmgate Café upstairs. Head Chef Ed Camlin gave us this recipe for our little book and it is the best.

METHOD

Put all the ingredients except the potatoes into a bowl and mix well. Set aside to allow the flavours to develop. Hold the green herbs until the last minute so that they stay nice and green.

Put the potatoes in a large saucepan with barely enough cold salted water to cover. Bring to the boil and cook over a medium heat for 10 minutes, or until the potatoes are cooked but firm. Drain and leave to cool slightly.

Lightly smash the potatoes and toss in the dressing, adding the green herbs. Serve immediately.

If you like, you can prepare everything in advance and combine them later. Add a little olive oil to a frying pan, add the dressing and potatoes and heat through – fold through the herbs at the very last minute.

SERVES 4

INGREDIENTS

900 g/2 lb potatoes, unpeeled

1 small head of cabbage, chopped

300 ml/10 fl oz milk

6 tbsp butter

salt and freshly ground black pepper

Colcannon

Colcannon, traditionally a Hallowe'en dish, is good at any time of the year and is best made with floury potatoes such as Home Guard, Kerr's Pinks or Golden Wonders.

METHOD

Cook the potatoes in a saucepan of lightly salted water for 30 minutes, or until just tender. Cook the cabbage in a small amount of boiling water for 4 minutes, or until just tender – do not allow it to overcook and become soggy. Drain the potatoes, then peel and mash them. Bring the milk to almost boiling and add enough to the potatoes to make a soft but not runny consistency. Add the cabbage, mix well, season to taste with salt and pepper and transfer to a warmed dish. Make a well in the centre, add the butter and serve immediately.

SERVES 4-6

INGREDIENTS

6 potatoes
1 large bunch of parsley
pinch of bicarbonate of soda
2 tbsp butter, plus extra to serve
1 small onion, finely chopped
125 ml/4 fl oz milk

Onion Colcannon

This old recipe for colcannon uses parsley and onion instead of cabbage or kale.

METHOD

Boil the potatoes and mash well. Tie the parsley in a bunch and place in a saucepan of boiling water with the bicarbonate of soda. Boil for 3 minutes and drain. Remove the stalks, chop the leaves well and add to the mashed potatoes. Put the butter, onion and milk into a small saucepan, bring to the boil and simmer for 5 minutes. Add to the potatoes and mix well with a fork. Serve in a warmed dish with a knob of butter in the centre.

SERVES 4-6

INGREDIENTS

900 g/2 lb floury
potatoes
115 g/4 oz large
spring onions
300 ml/10 fl oz milk
115 g/4 oz butter
salt and freshly
ground black pepper

Champ

Champ is cooked all over the country and,
like Colcannon, has many variations.
Traditionally, it is made using onion but
you can substitute a whole range of other
things such as young nettles, parsley, wild
garlic, leeks or herbs.

METHOD

Cook the potatoes in lightly salted boiling water for about
30 minutes until tender. Chop the spring onions, place in a
saucepan with half the milk and simmer for about 5 minutes.
Strain, reserving the milk. Peel the potatoes and mash them with
the spring onions, adding the reserved milk and as much of the
remaining milk as you need to make a soft, light mixture. Season
to taste with salt and pepper, transfer to a warmed dish, make a
well in the centre, add the butter and serve at once.

SERVES 4–6

INGREDIENTS

8 large old or new
potatoes

115 g/4 oz flour

1 tsp bicarbonate
of soda

225 ml/8 fl oz
milk

pinch of salt

2 tbsp butter, plus
extra to serve

Nancy's Boxty

My husband's aunt Nancy Geelen was from
the boxty stronghold of Leitrim and was
famous for her boxty. This is her recipe.

METHOD

Scrub the potatoes and peel them if they are old. Grate into
a large dish using the fine side of the grater. Drain the potato
into a clean tea towel to remove the excess liquid. Add the
flour, bicarbonate of soda, milk and salt and mix well with a
wooden spoon. Melt the butter in a heavy frying pan. When it is
bubbling, add the potato mixture. Cook, turning, until brown
on both sides. Serve at once with more butter.

SERVES 4-6

INGREDIENTS

900 g/2 lb floury potatoes

2 tsp plain white flour

butter or bacon fat, for frying

salt

Quick Boxty

This is a quick and easy pan recipe for a simple boxty.

METHOD

Scrub and grate the potatoes into a clean tea towel – you can peel them if you like but there is no need, unless the skin looks unpleasant. Leave to stand for a while, then drain off any liquid before adding the flour and salt to taste.

Pat the mixture into a 2–2.5-cm/¾–1-inch thick cake the diameter of your frying pan. Add some butter to the pan and heat until foaming, then add the boxty. Leave to cook for about 30 minutes, turning once, until golden on the base. Turn it by removing the pan from the heat, placing a large plate upside down on the pan and turning it over. Slip the boxty back into the pan and cook on the other side until golden.

SERVES 4-6

INGREDIENTS

4 garlic cloves, chopped

1 tbsp olive oil

1 tbsp butter, plus extra for greasing

1.1 kg/2 lb 8 oz potatoes, unpeeled and thinly sliced

salt and freshly ground black pepper

Sliced Potatoes with Garlic

These potatoes are quick to prepare and quick to cook; they're great when you are in a hurry. It takes 5 minutes to prepare, looks sophisticated and tastes good.

METHOD

Preheat the oven to 190°C/375°F/Gas Mark 5. Grease a 25-cm/10-inch pie dish or flan dish with butter. Put the garlic in a small saucepan with the olive oil and butter and heat until the butter has melted and is hot. Don't allow it to sizzle or brown.

Arrange the potatoes in the prepared dish in three layers, seasoning between each layer. Pour the garlic, butter and oil mixture evenly over the top. Bake in the preheated oven for 45 minutes, or until the top is golden.

SERVES 6

INGREDIENTS

900 g/2 lb new
potatoes
4 tbsp butter
salt and freshly
ground black pepper

Château Potatoes

This rich potato dish is easy to make. It
goes well with Sunday roasts, and is good
for other special occasions.

METHOD

Preheat the oven to 200°C/400°F/Gas Mark 6. Scrub the
potatoes and dry them well on a clean tea towel. Melt the
butter in a wide saucepan, add the potatoes and cook over a
medium heat, turning frequently, until they are brown. Add salt
and pepper to taste, transfer to a roasting tin and cook in the
preheated oven for 10–12 minutes. Serve in a warmed dish.

SERVES 4

INGREDIENTS

butter, for greasing
8 potatoes
225 ml/8 fl oz single cream
225 ml/8 fl oz buttermilk
2 tsp French mustard
115 g/4 oz white Cheddar cheese
30 g/1 oz freshly grated Parmesan cheese
salt and freshly ground black pepper

Potatoes with Buttermilk

A friend, Elaine Hartigan, serves this rich dish with bacon – a good match.

METHOD

Preheat the oven to 190°C/375°F/Gas Mark 5. Grease a baking dish with butter. Parboil the potatoes for about 15 minutes. Drain, peel and halve them, and place flat-side down in the prepared dish. Mix the cream, buttermilk and mustard in a bowl, season well and pour over the potatoes. Grate the Cheddar cheese on top, then sprinkle over the Parmesan cheese. Bake in the preheated oven for 30–40 minutes.

The buttermilk and cheese blend into the potatoes so they are deliciously crusty on top.

SERVES 4-6

INGREDIENTS

900 g/2 lb potatoes

225 g/8 oz field mushrooms

2 tbsp butter

2 tbsp plain flour

300 ml/10 fl oz milk

pinch of freshly grated nutmeg

2 tbsp cream or yogurt

salt and freshly ground black pepper

Potatoes and Mushrooms

Good tasty mushrooms are essential for this recipe.

METHOD

Peel and quarter the potatoes and trim the cut edges with a potato peeler. Cook gently in boiling water until just tender. Drain the water and reserve, and leave the potatoes to dry. Wipe the mushrooms clean, leaving the stalks on.

Heat the butter in a saucepan over a high heat, then add the mushrooms and toss. Mix in the flour, milk and 300 ml/10 fl oz of the reserved potato water. Season with salt and pepper to taste, bring to the boil and add the potatoes. Cover and cook for about 10 minutes. Stir in the nutmeg and cream just before serving.

SERVES 4

INGREDIENTS

350 g / 12 oz carrots, cut into 2.5-cm/ 1-inch lengths

550 g / 1 lb 4 oz potatoes, diced

2 tbsp butter

¼ tsp grated nutmeg

115 ml / 3¾ fl oz hot milk

salt and freshly ground black pepper

Puréed Potatoes and Carrots

This recipe is very light and makes an interesting alternative to mashed potatoes.

METHOD

Put the carrots and potatoes into a saucepan of lightly salted water. Bring to the boil and simmer for 15–20 minutes until tender. Be careful not to overcook. Purée the vegetables or put them through a coarse sieve. Return to a clean saucepan. Add the butter, nutmeg and salt and pepper to taste and heat over a medium heat, beating in the hot milk with a wooden spoon. Serve immediately.

SERVES 4

INGREDIENTS

butter, for greasing

115 g/4 oz cream cheese

115 g/4 oz Parmesan cheese or Gruyère cheese

150 ml/5 fl oz cream

3 eggs

60 ml/2 fl oz top-of-the-bottle full-cream milk

a pinch of chopped fresh rosemary or thyme

2 tsp freshly grated nutmeg

675 g/1 lb 8 oz potatoes

salt and freshly ground black pepper

Potato Gratin

Potato gratin made the following way can easily be served as a main course. It is rich and very good.

METHOD

Preheat the oven to 200°C/400°F/Gas Mark 6. Grease a gratin dish with butter. Beat the cream cheese, Parmesan cheese and cream together, then beat in the eggs. Add the milk and herbs, season to taste with salt and pepper and the nutmeg. Peel and grate the potatoes. Sprinkle with salt and pepper and leave to stand for 5–10 minutes. Drain off the liquid and put the potatoes into the prepared dish. Pour over the cheese and cream mixture and cook in the preheated oven for 40–45 minutes.

SERVES 6

INGREDIENTS

675 g/1 lb 8 oz
potatoes

85 g/3 oz strong
Cheddar cheese

85 g/3 oz chopped
cooked bacon or
ham (optional)

a few fresh herbs,
such as sage, thyme
and parsley

450 ml/16 fl oz milk

4 tbsp butter, plus
extra for greasing

salt and freshly
ground black pepper

Scalloped Potatoes

Bacon or ham make a great addition to
this recipe.

METHOD

Preheat the oven to 180°C/350°F/Gas Mark 4. Grease a baking
dish with butter. Scrub the potatoes and slice them thinly. Layer
them in the prepared dish. Add salt and pepper to taste, cheese,
bacon and herbs followed by another layer of potatoes. Repeat
each layer, finishing with a layer of potatoes. Add the milk, dot
with the butter and bake in the preheated oven for 45 minutes,
or until the potatoes are cooked and the top is crisp.

SERVES 4

INGREDIENTS

butter, for greasing
2 eggs
125 ml/4 fl oz milk
125 ml/4 fl oz cream
3 large garlic cloves, crushed
175 g/6 oz Cheddar cheese, grated
½ tsp grated nutmeg
900 g/2 lb potatoes, thinly sliced
4 spring onions, finely chopped
salt and freshly ground black pepper

Potatoes Layered with Cheese

A simply delicious version of potatoes dauphinoise, perfect for serving on special occasions.

METHOD

Preheat the oven to 180°C/350°F/Gas Mark 4. Grease a baking dish with butter. Beat the eggs with the milk, cream, garlic, half the cheese, the nutmeg and salt and pepper to taste. Add the potatoes and spring onions, then put the mixture into the prepared dish. Sprinkle the remaining cheese on top. Bake in the preheated oven for 40 minutes, taking care that the cheese on top does not burn.

SERVES 6

INGREDIENTS

oil, for greasing

675 g/1 lb 8 oz potatoes

2 tbsp butter

1 onion, finely chopped

2 tbsp snipped fresh chives

30 g/1 oz Cheddar cheese, grated

salt and freshly ground black pepper

Baked Potato Shapes

These are irresistible to adults and children alike. Using a scone or biscuit cutter, they can be made into any shape you wish.

METHOD

Preheat the oven to 220°C/425°F/Gas Mark 7. Grease a baking sheet with oil. Parboil the potatoes for about 15 minutes until almost tender. Leave to cool, then peel and grate them with a coarse grater. Melt the butter and cook the onion until they are soft but not brown. Mix with the potatoes, cheese, chives and salt and pepper to taste. Spoon 8 mounds or shapes of the mixture onto the prepared baking sheet. Bake in the preheated oven for about 15 minutes until they are golden and crispy on the outside.

SERVES 4

INGREDIENTS

675 g/1 lb 8 oz
small new potatoes

2 tbsp olive oil

55 g/2 oz freshly
grated Parmesan
cheese

salt and freshly
ground black pepper

Fried New Potatoes with Cheese

This is a great recipe, not unlike the roast potatoes with Parmesan, but they have quite a different flavour when cooked in the pan.

METHOD

Cook the potatoes in lightly salted boiling water for about 10 minutes until tender. Heat the oil in a large heavy-based frying pan, add the potatoes and toss in the oil for about 5 minutes. Stir in the cheese and cook for a further 1–2 minutes until the cheese begins to blend; if you cook it for too long the cheese will be tough. Season with a very little salt and pepper.

SERVES 4

INGREDIENTS

4 large potatoes
225 ml/8 fl oz
double cream
⅓ tsp freshly grated
nutmeg
pinch of cayenne
pepper
115 g/4 oz spring
onions, chopped
salt

Potatoes in Cream Sauce

This recipe is a quick accompaniment to make, which goes well with fairly plain dishes.

METHOD

Peel and rinse the potatoes. Slice into quarters lengthways and cut into 2.5-cm/1-inch lengths. Put the potatoes into a saucepan of lightly salted water and bring to the boil. Simmer for about 5 minutes, then drain. Add the cream, nutmeg, cayenne pepper, spring onions, and salt to taste. Bring to the boil, cover and cook for about 4 minutes until almost tender. Season with salt and boil uncovered for 1 minute, or until the cream has thickened.

SERVES 4

INGREDIENTS

900 g/2 lb potatoes
2 large onions, thinly sliced
225 ml/8 fl oz Smithwicks ale or lager
4 tbsp butter, very cold, plus extra for greasing
150 ml/5 fl oz cream
salt and freshly ground black pepper

Potatoes Baked in Smithwicks

Potatoes with beer is not a combination that normally springs to mind, but this is good!

METHOD

Preheat the oven to 220°C/425°F/Gas Mark 7. Grease a baking dish with butter. Scrub the potatoes well and slice them thinly. Place alternate slices of onion and potato in the prepared dish, packed closely together. Salt each layer lightly. Add the beer and shavings of butter, evenly distributed. Bake in the preheated oven for 10 minutes, then reduce the oven temperature to 180°C/350°F/Gas Mark 4 and cook for a further 40 minutes.

About 10 minutes before the end of cooking pour the cream evenly over the top, then return to the oven.

SERVES 4

INGREDIENTS

4 large potatoes, cut into quarters

2 tbsp butter

30 g/1 oz freshly grated Parmesan cheese

2 eggs, separated, whites lightly beaten

large pinch of nutmeg

dried breadcrumbs, for coating

groundnut oil, for frying

salt and freshly ground black pepper

Potato Parmesan

This strong, rich potato dish is excellent with game.

METHOD

Cook the potatoes in lightly salted boiling water until tender. Drain and mash. Add the butter, cheese, egg yolks, nutmeg, and salt and pepper to taste and mix well. When cool, shape into 5-cm/2-inch rounds. Coat with lightly beaten egg white, then turn in the breadcrumbs to coat. Heat some oil in a frying pan, add the rounds and cook for about 5 minutes, turning once, until golden. Remove from the pan, drain on warmed kitchen paper and serve immediately.

SERVES 4

INGREDIENTS

2 tbsp olive oil

1 large onion, finely chopped

1 garlic clove

4 potatoes, very thinly sliced

400 ml/14 fl oz chicken stock

½ tsp mixed chopped fresh sage and fresh thyme

salt

Baker's Potatoes

This recipe is very good with roast pork that has been prepared with a stuffing using the same herbs.

METHOD

Preheat the oven to 200°C/400°F/Gas Mark 6. Heat the oil in a shallow, heavy-based ovenproof frying pan, stir in the onion and soften over a low heat. Mash the garlic with a little salt and add it to the onion with the potato slices, coating the slices with the oil. Barely cover with the stock. Scatter the herbs on top, cover with foil and bake in the preheated oven for about 40 minutes.

SERVES 4–6

INGREDIENTS

900 g/2 lb new
potatoes
4-6 tbsp butter
1 large fresh parsley
sprig, chopped
salt and freshly
ground black pepper

New Potatoes in Parsley Butter

Another simple but terrific potato recipe.
The parsley butter gives the potatoes a
melt-in-the-mouth flavour.

METHOD

Cook the potatoes in a large saucepan of lightly salted boiling
water for about 15 minutes until tender, then drain. Meanwhile,
melt the butter in a small saucepan, add the parsley, salt and
pepper, and stir well. Place the potatoes in a warmed serving
dish, pour the parsley butter over and serve.

SERVES 4

INGREDIENTS

4–5 tbsp olive oil
5 garlic cloves
425 ml/15 fl oz
water
900 g/2 lb potatoes
4 bay leaves

Potatoes with Garlic and Bay Leaves

The bay leaves in this recipe give a lovely flavour which seems to seep through in the cooking.

METHOD

Preheat the oven to 200°C/400°F/Gas Mark 6. Use some of the oil to grease a baking dish. Put the garlic into a saucepan with the water, bring to a simmer, then simmer for 15 minutes. Lift out the garlic, reserving the cooking water, push the soft flesh from the skin, and purée through a sieve back into the water.

Meanwhile, slice the potatoes thinly and leave to dry. Pack half the potatoes into the prepared dish, then add the bay leaves and the remaining potatoes. Pour over the garlic water to cover them, and drizzle the remaining oil on top. Cook in the preheated oven for 45–50 minutes.

SERVES 4–6

INGREDIENTS

2 large garlic cloves
4 tbsp butter, plus
extra for greasing
1.1 kg/2 lb 8 oz
potatoes, thinly
sliced
600–900 ml/1–1½
pints cream
salt and freshly
ground black pepper

Garlic Potatoes with Cream

Denise Barnes gave me this recipe and it is unlikely you could find anything with so many calories per gram or so indulgently delicious.

METHOD

Preheat the oven to 180°C/350°F/Gas Mark 4. Grease a baking dish with butter. Finely chop the garlic and mix with the butter. Layer the potatoes and garlic butter and salt and pepper to taste in the prepared dish, until all the potatoes are used up. Pour over enough cream to cover the potatoes, and cook in the preheated oven for 1–1¼ hours, until the potatoes are tender and the top is golden brown.

SERVES 4

INGREDIENTS

4 large floury potatoes, such as Queens

3 tbsp oil

1 garlic clove, crushed

450 g/1 lb frozen spinach, thawed and drained

2 tbsp yogurt

55 g/2 oz dry breadcrumbs

2 tbsp butter, melted

Spinach and Yogurt Potato Skins

Spinach, potatoes and yoghurt are so good together. This is a real favourite.

METHOD

Preheat the oven to 220°C/425°F/Gas Mark 7. Prick the potatoes, place them on a baking tray and bake in the preheated oven for about 1 hour. Cut into quarters and spoon out the flesh into a bowl, leaving a little on the skins. Brush the skins with oil and return them to the oven to cook for a further 10 minutes.

Heat 2 tablespoons of the oil in a frying pan, add the garlic and drained spinach, and cook for about 3 minutes, stirring constantly. Remove from the heat, add the potato flesh, yogurt and half the breadcrumbs, and leave the mixture to cool a little. Add the remaining breadcrumbs to the melted butter and set aside. Spoon the spinach mixture into the potato skins and sprinkle with the breadcrumbs and butter mixture. Return them to the oven and cook for 10 minutes, or until lightly browned.

SERVES 4

SALADS

Potatoes are delicious when combined with all sorts of salad ingredients, adding body and texture to fresh green leaves and raw vegetables. They also make substantial salads in their own right, perhaps warm with an oil-based dressing and topped with bacon bits, or mixed with a home-made mayonnaise studded with fresh chives.

Duine de chinéal na bhfataí beaga, duine gan suim.
A person similar to small potatoes is not an interesting person.

Irish Saying

INGREDIENTS

675 g/1 lb 8 oz new
potatoes
1 tsp chopped fresh
mint
6 tbsp vegetable oil
2 tbsp extra virgin
olive oil
2 tbsp red wine
vinegar
1 tbsp Irish mustard
1 tbsp snipped
chives
mixed salad leaves
salt and freshly
ground black pepper

Potato and Chive Salad

A mix of summer salad leaves is best in
this dish, but any available green leaves
will do, the fresher the better.

METHOD

Cover the potatoes with lightly salted boiling water and add the
mint. Bring to the boil, drain and cut into bite-sized pieces. Set
aside to cool.

Whisk the vegetable oil, olive oil, vinegar and mustard together
and add salt and pepper to taste. Pour the dressing over the
potatoes, add the chives, toss with the salad leaves and serve at
once.

SERVES 4

INGREDIENTS

900 g/2 lb new
potatoes

6 tbsp extra virgin
olive oil

1 onion, chopped

generous sprig of
fresh rosemary

1 egg yolk

2 tbsp vinegar

2 tomatoes

12 stoned black
olives

85 g/3 oz mature
Cheddar cheese,
grated

salt and freshly
ground black pepper

Potato Salad with Rosemary and Cheese

This recipe works well accompanied by a good green salad of fresh leaves.

METHOD

Cook the potatoes in lightly salted boiling water until tender, then drain. Heat the oil in a pan, add the onion and half the rosemary leaves, and cook until the onion is lightly browned. Drain the oil and set aside to cool.

Beat the egg yolk until frothy, then slowly pour in the oil, taking care not to curdle it; add the vinegar and salt and pepper to taste. Chop the tomatoes and the potatoes and place in a large salad bowl. Add the onions, olives and cheese, pour the dressing over the salad and sprinkle with the remaining rosemary. Serve while still warm.

SERVES 4

INGREDIENTS

675 g/1 lb 8 oz new potatoes

2 tbsp extra virgin olive oil

2 tbsp sunflower oil

1 tbsp red wine vinegar

1 garlic clove, crushed

handful of fresh mint leaves, chopped

1 tbsp snipped fresh chives

salt and freshly ground black pepper

New Potato Salad with Mint and Chives

The herbs in this recipe blend well with the French dressing although you can, of course, substitute your own favourite herbs. Choose similar sized potatoes.

METHOD

Steam the potatoes for about 10 minutes until tender. Mix together the olive oil, sunflower oil, vinegar, garlic, and salt and pepper to taste. When the potatoes are cooked toss them in the dressing, add the mint and chives and serve.

SERVES 4

INGREDIENTS

675 g/1 lb 8 oz new potatoes

2 tbsp extra virgin olive oil

2 tbsp red wine vinegar

3 slices Parma ham

1 tbsp snipped fresh chives or finely chopped spring onions

3–4 sprigs of fresh parsley, chopped

salt and freshly ground black pepper

Warm Potato Salad with Parma Ham and Parsley

The Parma ham gives this salad a lovely flavour. Do leave the warm potatoes to soak up the dressing for ten minutes or so before serving.

METHOD

Cook the potatoes in lightly salted boiling water until tender. Meanwhile, mix the oil and vinegar together. Chop the ham into small strips and put it in a large serving dish. Add the oil and vinegar, chives, and salt and pepper to taste. Add the potatoes with the parsley and toss carefully to coat in the dressing. Leave to stand for at least 5 minutes to allow the potatoes to absorb the dressing, then serve.

SERVES 4

INGREDIENTS

675 g/1 lb 8 oz
small new potatoes

4 handfuls of fresh
flat-leaf parsley,
roughly chopped

55 g/2 oz Parmesan
cheese from the
block

Dressing

1 small garlic clove,
mashed almost to
liquid with the edge
of a knife

2 tsp white wine

3 tbsp olive oil

1 tbsp sunflower oil

salt and freshly
ground black pepper

Potato and Parsley Salad

A lovely fresh salad with a delicious French
dressing that will bring the taste of spring
to your table.

METHOD

Steam the potatoes until they are just tender, then leave to cool
slightly. Make the dressing by mixing all the dressing ingredients
in a large salad bowl. Toss the potatoes in the dressing with the
parsley, making sure they are well coated. Use a potato peeler to
shave the cheese over the salad, then serve.

SERVES 4

INGREDIENTS

12 new potatoes

6 streaky bacon rashers

2 tbsp extra virgin olive oil

2 tbsp white wine vinegar

1 large handful of rocket

4 tbsp snipped fresh chives

Warm Potato Salad with Crispy Bacon and Rocket

The vinegar is important in this recipe to bring out the flavour of the ingredients.

METHOD

Cook the potatoes in boiling water until tender, drain and set aside. Chop the bacon and cook in a large frying pan over a high heat until crisp. Drain on kitchen paper. Mix the oil, vinegar, rocket, chives and bacon in a large serving dish. Add the potatoes, stir and serve.

SERVES 4

INGREDIENTS

450 g/1 lb small new potatoes, halved

4 tbsp lemon juice, or to taste

4 tbsp olive oil

1 small cucumber, chopped

1 celery stick, chopped

4 large spring onions

115 g/4 oz fresh parsley, chopped

3 tbsp chopped fresh mint

salt and freshly ground black pepper

Minted Potato Salad

This lovely salad can be made a little in advance and kept in the fridge. You could use a little less lemon if you find it a bit sharp.

METHOD

Cook the potatoes in boiling water until just tender, drain, dry and cut in half. Mix the lemon juice and oil with salt and pepper to taste in a large salad bowl. Add the remaining ingredients and mix well, making sure that the mint and parsley are well distributed. Taste for seasoning and serve.

SERVES 4

INGREDIENTS

450 g/1 lb new potatoes

30 g/1 oz hazelnuts, toasted and roughly chopped

2 tbsp hazelnut oil

2 tbsp olive oil

200 g/7 oz Gorgonzola or similar cheese

salt and freshly ground black pepper

Delicious Cheese and Potato Salad

This recipe is made with Gorgonzola or any creamy, strong cheese. Cashel Blue works really well.

METHOD

Cook the potatoes in lightly salted boiling water until tender. Drain and cut in half. Meanwhile, mix the hazelnuts with the hazelnut oil and olive oil. Roughly chop the cheese and add to the hazelnuts with the potatoes and mix well. Season carefully and serve immediately.

SERVES 4

INGREDIENTS

675 g/1 lb 8 oz firm
potatoes such as
King Edwards or
Roosters
salt

Dressing
1 tbsp anchovy paste
4-6 anchovy fillets
½ small onion, finely
chopped
1-2 garlic cloves
1 tbsp capers
150 ml/5 fl oz white
wine

Potato Salad with Anchovies

If you like anchovies you will love this
dish. As always with anchovies, watch the
seasoning – they are very salty and the
chances are that you will not need to add
salt when it comes to seasoning.

METHOD

Cook the potatoes in lightly salted water until tender. Drain,
peel and cut into cubes. Meanwhile, put the anchovy paste into
a bowl, add the anchovies with their oil and mix well with a
wooden spoon or salad server. Add the onion, garlic, capers and
wine. Add the potatoes to the dressing while they are still warm.
Cover and leave to stand for at least 15 minutes before serving.

SERVES 4

POTATO CAKES

Potato cakes are a very traditional Irish dish, good for breakfast, lunch or any other time and a great way to use up leftover potatoes. There are many variations, some very simple and some quite rich.

Bheadh ne fátaí nite, bruite agus ite agat fad a bheadh an Ciarríoch ag rá prátaí!
You would have the potatoes washed, boiled and eaten while a Kerryman is saying prátaí!

The word fátaí is the Connemara word for potato so a joke between Connemara and Munster Irish.

INGREDIENTS

225 g/8 oz mashed potatoes
115 g/4 oz flour
115 g/4 oz softened butter, plus extra for frying and to serve
salt and freshly ground black pepper

Simple Potato Cakes

These are the simplest version of this delicious way of dealing with all those leftover mashed potatoes.

METHOD

Mash the potatoes with the flour, butter and seasoning. Knead together until it has a rough dough-like consistency. Roll out and slice or cut into 10-cm/4-inch rounds. Heat some butter in a frying pan, add the rounds and fry until they are golden brown, turning once. You may need to add a little more butter when you turn them. Serve immediately with a knob of butter melting on top.

SERVES 4

INGREDIENTS

225 g/8 oz mashed
potatoes

115 g/4 oz plain
flour

85 g/3 oz butter,
plus extra for frying

40 g/1½ oz freshly
grated Parmesan
cheese

salt and freshly
ground black pepper

Parmesan Potato Cakes

**Parmesan is not a traditional addition to
potato cakes but it works really well. We
often have these for lunch served with a
simple parsley or green salad.**

METHOD

Put the potatoes, flour, butter, cheese and salt and pepper to
taste in a bowl. Knead to a rough dough-like consistency and
roll. Cut into shapes. Melt some butter in a frying pan, add the
shapes and fry until golden, turning once, adding more butter
if needed. Serve immediately.

SERVES 4

INGREDIENTS

225 g/8 oz mashed potatoes

about 3 tbsp flour

1 large egg, separated

2 tbsp melted butter

2 tbsp chopped mixed peel (optional)

pinch of salt

Theodora FitzGibbon's Potato Cake

This recipe comes from Theodora FitzGibbon's *Irish Traditional Food*; she says it is a very old country method. Theodora's recipe uses mixed peel, but my children won't eat it with peel so I either substitute another dried fruit or omit it. I prefer it plain with butter.

METHOD

Mash the potatoes in a bowl with sufficient flour to form a firm dough. Blend in just over half the butter. Beat the egg yolk and egg white separately. Add the beaten egg yolk to the mixture, then add the stiffly beaten egg white. Season well and shape into a round cake the diameter of your frying pan. Add the remaining butter to a heavy-based frying pan and add the cake. Cover and cook for about 30 minutes over a medium heat. Serve hot.

SERVES 4

INGREDIENTS

675 g/1 lb 8 oz
potatoes
150 ml/5 fl oz
cream
115 g/4 oz butter
3 tbsp chopped
onion
3 celery sticks,
chopped
4–6 tbsp Gruyère
cheese, grated
pinch of cayenne
pepper
pinch of freshly
grated nutmeg
salt

Potato, Gruyère and Celery Cake

This very rich cake is full of flavour and would be delicious with roast meat as part of a big meal, or with some tomatoes and red peppers roasted in olive oil.

METHOD

Cook the potatoes in lightly salted boiling water for 15–20 minutes until just tender. Drain and mash with the cream. Meanwhile, melt half the butter in a heavy-based frying pan, add the onion and celery and cook until they are transparent. Add to the potatoes. Mix in the cheese and season with the cayenne pepper, nutmeg and salt, to taste.

Melt the remaining butter in a separate frying pan, add the potato and celery mixture and spread into a flat cake. Cook for about 15 minutes, then cover the pan with a plate and turn it upside down. Slip the cake back onto the pan, add the remaining butter and cook for a further 10 minutes until golden. Cut into wedges and serve at once.

SERVES 4

INGREDIENTS

900 g/2 lb potatoes
55 g/2 oz self-
raising flour
1 egg, beaten
groundnut oil, for
frying
3 tbsp caster sugar
mixed with 1 tsp
cinnamon
salt and freshly
ground black pepper

Latkes

Latkes are a kind of potato pancake, often flavoured with other ingredients.

METHOD

Peel the potatoes and grate into cold water. Strain and squeeze in a clean tea towel to get the water out. Place in a bowl, add the flour, beaten egg and salt and pepper to taste and mix well. Heat the oil in a heavy-based frying pan and carefully drop a tablespoon of the mixture into the oil; fry until golden, turning once. Drain well on warmed kitchen paper. Dust with the sugar and cinnamon mixture and serve hot.

SERVES 4

INGREDIENTS

450 g/1 lb freshly
made mashed potato
1 heaped tbsp butter
2 tsp white
granulated sugar
pinch of ginger
3 tbsp plain flour
900 g/2 lb cooking
apples, peeled and
sliced
1 tbsp soft light
brown sugar, for
dusting

Potato and Apple Cake

This is one of the wonderful Theordora
FitzGibbon's recipes.

METHOD

Preheat the oven to 180°C/350°F/Gas Mark 4. Blend the potato
with the butter, white sugar and ginger. Add enough flour to
make a workable dough, and knead until smooth. Roll out into
two rounds, one a little bigger than the other. Put the larger
round on a piece of greaseproof paper, cover with the sliced
apple and sprinkle with brown sugar. Dampen the edges of the
dough and put the smaller round on top, pressing down to seal
the edges. Prick all over with a fork and make a small cut in the
middle. Cook in the preheated oven for about 35 minutes until
a nice golden brown. Serve hot, dusted with brown sugar.

SERVES 4

INGREDIENTS

450 g/1 lb potatoes,
preferably Queens

80 g/3 oz butter

1 spring onion,
chopped

8 g/¼ oz fresh
thyme

20 g/1 oz snipped
fresh chives

plain flour, for
dusting

2 eggs, lightly
beaten

breadcrumbs for
coating, preferably
Panko for extra
crunch

groundnut oil, for
deep-frying

salt and white
pepper

Nash 19 Breakfast Potato Cakes

Everything from Nash 19 in Cork is
delicious and this recipe is no exception
– these potato cakes are particularly good
with smoked salmon or poached eggs.

METHOD

Peel, boil and mash the potatoes until smooth. Add the butter,
spring onion, thyme and chives with a pinch of salt and pepper
to taste.

Shape the mixture into rounds. Lightly coat with flour, carefully
dip in the egg and then roll in the breadcrumbs.

Heat enough oil for deep-frying to 180°C/350°F, add the potato
cakes and fry until golden. Serve at once.

MAKES 6

INGREDIENTS

900 g/2 lb potatoes, peeled and diced
125 ml/4 fl oz milk
½ onion, finely chopped or grated
55 g/2 oz plain flour
2 tsp salt
2 egg whites
groundnut oil, for frying

Potato Pancakes

These are much nicer than they sound and are easy to make. Serve them for lunch with apple sauce and a green salad.

METHOD

Grate the potatoes with a fine grater onto a clean tea towel and leave for about 10 minutes so that the liquid can run off. Place in a bowl, stir in the milk and add the onion, flour and salt. Mix very well, add the egg whites and mix again. Leave to stand for 10 minutes.

Heat some oil in a frying pan – be generous with the oil, you need lots to cook this properly. Spoon in about 2 tablespoons of the batter to make a small thickish pancake. You can cook as many of these together as your pan allows. After 2–3 minutes, turn them and fry for a further 3 minutes. Transfer to a warmed dish lined with kitchen paper to drain, then serve.

SERVES 4–6

INGREDIENTS

650 g/1 lb 7 oz raw or parboiled potatoes, grated

2 spring onions, finely chopped

1 tbsp chopped fresh herbs, such as parsley or rosemary

2 tbsp olive oil

4 tbsp butter

salt and freshly ground black pepper

green salad, to serve

Potato Rösti with Spring Onions and Herbs

Rösti can be made with raw or parboiled potatoes. If you use raw potatoes, just peel and grate them into a clean tea towel and squeeze well to get rid of any excess starch and moisture. Otherwise, scrub the potatoes and cook in boiling salted water for about 10 minutes. Leave to cool a little, then grate. Rösti works well as a main course but also as a side dish.

METHOD

Mix the grated potato with the spring onions and herbs. Heat the oil in a heavy-based frying pan until very hot, then pour off and wipe out the pan with kitchen paper. Reduce the heat and add half the butter and then the potato mixture. Press down – the potato should be about 2.5 cm/1 inch thick. Cook for about 10 minutes. Cover with a plate, then turn the pan upside down. Melt the remaining butter in the pan, then slide the rösti back onto the pan and cook on the other side.

Serve piping hot with a green salad.

SERVES 4

INGREDIENTS

675 g/1 lb 8 oz waxy potatoes

2 tbsp cooking oil

4 tbsp butter, plus extra if needed

salt and freshly ground black pepper

Rösti

A delicious way to cook potatoes! You can substitute half the potatoes with celeriac, courgettes or parsnips.

METHOD

Parboil the potatoes for about 15 minutes, or until almost tender. Leave to cool, then peel them and grate them with a coarse grater. Meanwhile, heat the oil in a heavy-based frying pan. Leave to stand for a while, then pour off the oil and wipe out the pan with kitchen paper. Add half the butter to the pan and heat over a medium heat until melted, then add the potatoes in a 2.5-cm/1-inch layer. Sprinkle with salt and pepper. Press the potatoes into the pan with a flat spatula and cook for 10 minutes.

When the potatoes are golden brown, cover the pan with a plate and quickly turn the pan upside down onto the plate. Return the pan to the heat and slip the pancake back onto it. Add the remaining butter around the edge of the pan, allowing it to melt into the potato. Add more butter if you need to. Continue to cook, pressing it down occasionally until it is ready. Transfer to a warmed plate, slice into wedges and serve.

SERVES 4

INGREDIENTS

900 g/2 lb potatoes

900 g/2 lb celeriac

2 garlic cloves, crushed

pinch of freshly ground nutmeg

85 g/3 oz butter, melted, plus extra for greasing

salt and freshly ground black pepper

chopped fresh parsley or snipped fresh chives, to garnish

Potato and Celeriac Galette

This dish is quite delicious - even those who resist celeriac love it.

METHOD

Preheat the oven to 200°C/ 400°F/Gas Mark 6. Grease and base-line two 20-cm/8-inch round tins. Peel the potatoes and celeriac and slice very thinly. Layer them in the base of the prepared tins with the garlic, nutmeg and salt and pepper to taste, pressing down firmly as you layer. The tins should be full. Pour half the butter on each one. Cover with kitchen foil and cook in the preheated oven for about 1 hour, or until cooked. Turn out onto a warmed plate, garnish with parsley and serve.

SERVES 4

For permission to reproduce copyright photographs,
the publisher gratefully acknowledges the following:

p1 Shutterstock/Lestertair
p3 Shutterstock/zi3000
p8 Shutterstock/Rihardzz
p10 Shutterstock/
Catherine Jones
p12 Shutterstock/Jose Gil
p13 Shutterstock/
Jane McIlroy
p15 Shutterstock/
Semmick Photo
p17 Shutterstock/travellight
p19 Shutterstock/
HandmadePictures
p21 Ben Potter
p23 Ben Potter
p25 Shutterstock/
Elena Veselova
p27 Ben Potter
p29 Shutterstock/Yu Zu
p31 Ben Potter
p33 Shutterstock/keko64
p35 Shutterstock/carpaumar
p37 Ben Potter
p39 Shutterstock/Shebeko
p41 Shutterstock/
Successo Images
p43 Shutterstock/
Moving Moment
p45 Shutterstock/daffodilred
p47 Shutterstock/tonfon
p49 Shutterstock/
Patryk Kosmider
p51 Shutterstock/koss13
p53 Shutterstock/MaraZe
p55 Ben Potter
p57 Shutterstock/
Peredniankina
p59 Ben Potter
p61 Shutterstock/Joe Gough

p63 Ben Potter
p65 Shutterstock/
Olha Afanasieva
p67 Shutterstock/zi3000
p69 Ben Potter
p71 Ben Potter
p73 Ben Potter
p75 Ben Potter
p77 Shutterstock/Timolina
p79 Shutterstock/
MS Photographic
p81 Shutterstock/
Dmytro Mykhailov
p83 Ben Potter
p85 Ben Potter
p87 Ben Potter
p89 Ben Potter
p91 Ben Potter
p93 Shutterstock/
Pierre Leclerc
p95 Shutterstock/
Violeta Pasat
p97 Ben Potter
p99 Ben Potter
p101 Ben Potter
p103 Ben Potter
p105 Shutterstock/Fanfo
p107 Ben Potter
p109 Shutterstock/sta
p111 Ben Potter
p113 Shutterstock/
Robyn Mackenzie
p115 Shutterstock/vsl
p117 Ben Potter
p119 Shutterstock/
Robin Stewart
p121 Shutterstock/
Margouillat Photo
p123 Ben Potter

p125 Ben Potter
p127 Ben Potter
p129 Ben Potter
p129 Ben Potter
p131 Shutterstock/koss13
p133 Ben Potter
p135 Shutterstock/
Robcartorres
p137 Shutterstock/kuvona
p139 Shutterstock/
Marzia Giacobbe
p141 Shutterstock/EWETOO
p143 Ben Potter
p145 Ben Potter
p147 Ben Potter
p149 Ben Potter
p151 Ben Potter
p153 Ben Potter
p155 Ben Potter
p157 Shutterstock/
Martin Turzak
p159 Ben Potter
p161 Ben Potter
p163 Ben Potter
p165 Shutterstock/
Monkey Business Images
p167 Ben Potter
p169 Ben Potter
p171 Ben Potter
p173 Shutterstock/ Fanfo
p175 Shutterstock/Joerg Beuge
p177 Ben Potter
p179 Ben Potter
p181 Ben Potter
p183 Ben Potter
p185 Ben Potter
p187 Shutterstock/Wiktory
p189 Shutterstock/ Joshua
Resnick

p191 Ben Potter
p192 Ben Potter
p195 Ben Potter
p197 Ben Potter
p199 Ben Potter
p201 Ben Potter
p203 Ben Potter
p205 Ben Potter
p207 Ben Potter
p209 Ben Potter
p211 Ben Potter
p213 Shutterstock/
Gerardo Borbolla
p215 Ben Potter
p217 Ben Potter
p219 Ben Potter
p221 Ben Potter
p223 Ben Potter
p225 Ben Potter
p227 Ben Potter
p229 Ben Potter
p231 Ben Potter
p233 Shutterstock/
Richard Semik
p235 Shutterstock/
Margouillat Photo
p237 Shutterstock/
Joerg Beuge
p239 Ben Potter
p241 Ben Potter
p243 Ben Potter
p245 Shutterstock/
Brent Hofacker
p247 Ben Potter
p249 Shutterstock/Sea Wave
p251 Ben Potter
p253 Shutterstock/zkruger
p254 Ben Potter
Patterns: Shutterstock/
Nataliia Kucherenkoai